# plain & simple

11 knits to wear every day

quince&co.

Quince & Co
quinceandco.com

ISBN 978-0-9979187-1-7

Printed in the United States.

# contents

# introduction

Thinking up a sweater collection is a bit like writing a first sentence: Sometimes it comes along easily, other times it's a matter of fits and starts—and there's a lot of sleeping on it.

*Plain & Simple* had a somewhat reluctant first-sentence beginning. It began with one sweater, Ash, an oversized, pocketed pullover that was meant to be a one-off, not the start of a collection. I can't remember where the idea for this piece came from. It may be that my daughter was visiting and wore something wide and swingy and I was taken with it. Perhaps it was a photo I saw somewhere that sparked the idea. I'm not sure. But something prompted the notion of a sweater wide, wide, wide, with swing and drape. Around the same time, (and, really, always) I was wanting to knit with Owl, our lofty wool/alpaca blend, in one of the undyed natural colors. From there came the details: A close neck and fitted sleeves to balance the width, a bit of brioche stitch for texture, deep borders, and pockets.

Whatever yarn I'm currently knitting with becomes my favorite yarn. So while I worked on Ash, another Owl idea began a slow percolation—something more fitted, but, like Ash, basic and unfussy, something that would show off Owl's sweet nature, its heathery face, and soft hand. This next piece, Oak, is an almost-square pullover, closer to the body but still relaxed with another close neck and somewhat fitted sleeves, and a small pocket for detail.

Still enjoying Owl and its natural palette and wanting more brioche on the needle (brioche and its variations are especially pretty in Owl), Maple came forward: A little open cardigan finished at center front with a wide border in plush half-brioche rib.

By this time, of course, a book was beginning to take shape: Basic sweaters that are straightforward knitting and wearing and all worked in one of Owl's off-the-animal colorways.

And I had another reason for wanting to design a group of sweaters: Lately I've been experimenting with a sweater construction that's new to me—the dolman—worked in a hybrid way, body bottom-up, sleeves top-down. The body is worked to the armhole, then stitches are cast on at each end of the needle in a modified dolman style, then the sweater continues to the shoulder, with sleeves neatly picked up and knitted down from the armhole edge. What I love about this construction is the smooth shoulder line, uninterrupted by a set-in sleeve or the diagonal line of a raglan. It's perfect for knitted fabric, which stretches smoothly over the curve of the shoulder. Letting the fabric of the sweater body roll over the top of the arm to an armhole opening below the shoulder creates a smooth, uninterrupted line that takes full advantage of the gentle give of knitted fabric and makes a graceful garment that takes its form from the body underneath.

Furthermore, this dolman method is an easy knit. It avoids a shaped armhole and pesky sleeve cap. As in drop-sleeve construction, the armhole opening is straight, which makes it easy to pick up stitches around the opening and knit the sleeve down to the cuff—a move we all like because it allows for sleeve width and length adjustment as you go. Unlike drop-sleeve construction, however, the armhole isn't dictated by the width of the sweater, it can fall wherever you like it, wherever it flatters. The only seaming in this dolman-like construction is a three-needle bind off at the shoulder—some would call that more knitting than sewing.

You'll see a lot of stockinette stitch in these pieces, because I like to do other things while I knit, watch a movie, listen to a podcast, or read a book, all of which I can easily do when I'm simply knitting or purling. You'll also see brioche and half brioche patterns here, because these are my go-to rib variations. I love the soft, three-dimensional depth of brioche rib and the plump, rounded stitches in half brioche.

oak
in papuan

# introduction continued

I've included a modified round-yoke sweater with interest in the shoulder area created by a two-color slip stitch pattern. Slipped stitches are an often overlooked method for adding more colors to your work without having to carry yarn and knit with more than one strand in a given row.

And because the Owl natural palette is so perfect for color patterns, a round-yoke colorwork pullover found its way into the mix. I love the drama of light and dark in this palette of warm, earth tones. For simplicity——and drama——the pullover is worked in just two colors: almost-white Snowy, and Togian, a warm, chocolate brown.

We've named the sweaters in this book after trees. It seemed a fitting thing to do given that they're knitted in colors that are shorn from sheep and alpaca, nature's palette, for me, of irresistible earthy tones, conjuring the colors of wood.

What else? I've long been interested in what makes a favorite sweater. In Maine——where nights get cold, no matter the season——sweaters, in general, are in a good position to be a favorite garment. A warm wool pullover with forgiving stitches is a comfort. When I was pregnant with my two children I wore a colorful patterned V-neck sweater knitted by someone in Uruguay. It stretched to accommodate my belly and in almost every photo taken of me during that period of my life, I'm wearing it.

In the next period, and to this day——forgive me, Dear Knitter——the sweater I most often reach for is a man's crewneck that I bought many years ago at a J. Crew outlet. I know, I know——my favorite sweater should be handknitted. What the heck am I thinking?

Therefore, this book.

It might be that one or more of these sweaters will come home with me and finally supplant my ratty crew neck, to become my new favorite sweater.

Pam

**aspen**
in snowy & albertine

# owl

The sweaters in this book were designed around a specific yarn, *Owl*, from Quince & Co. Not that these pieces can't be made in other yarns. They most certainly can. But because I'm partial to this lovely blend of wool and alpaca, and the earthy, natural shades it comes in, I designed the sweaters in this book to take full advantage of the yarn's great qualities: Its softness, loft, and muted colors.

I love the range of natural, undyed colors in Owl. Alpaca fiber comes in 22 different shades, blue-black through brown-black, cool-to-warm browns, fawn, white, silver-grey, and rose-grey, all in various lights and darks——these are the colors right off the animal. Because Owl is a blend of wool and alpaca, the shades are heathered when the fibers are mixed with undyed white and brown wool. Is it tricky to duplicate these shades year after year? Yes. And our color line has expanded unintentionally because the exact fiber color varies from season to season; a bale of true black alpaca one year might be closer to a deep charcoal the next. And even with a recipe, the final blend is never the exact match of the original. At the beginning, we made new colors from our misses. These days we tolerate more variation between batches——we have to——but we're also getting better at duplication from batch to batch. Working with natural fibers means having to embrace change and variation, like most things in life.

Owl holds a special place in my heart for another reason. Anyone who's worked with alpaca knows just how lovely, warm, and soft it can be. But you may also have experienced alpaca's propensity to hang——and hang and hang——stretching down in the direction of your shoes. This slinky weight isn't necessarily a given. Alpaca is a hollow fiber, which means that there's air in the core. How much air you squeeze out or encourage in makes all the difference in the final yarn. In a spinning system that lines up the fibers so they are parallel to each other and squeezes them together, you push out the air and create a lank, inelastic yarn. However, if you spin alpaca on another system that throws the fibers together willy-nilly and incorporates air between them, you make a yarn buoyant and light; add wool to the mix for elasticity and bounce, and Voilà!

You have lovely, lofty Owl.

# sweaters

# ash

*yarn:* owl
*color:* elf

# chestnut

*yarn:* owl
*color:* tawny

# birch

*yarn:* owl
*colors:* togian & snowy

# oak

*yarn:* owl
*color:* papuan

# willow
*yarn:* owl
*color:* buru

# aspen

*yarn:* owl
*colors:* snowy & albertine

# larch

*yarn:* owl
*color:* albertine

# walnut

*yarn:* owl
*color:* sokoke

# maple

*yarn:* owl
*color:* barred

# balsam

*yarn:* owl
*color:* taiga

# shadbush

*yarn:* owl
*colors:* togian & snowy

# patterns

# ash

Ash is extra wide. Handy pockets are set into the sweater's deep half-brioche stitch border. To balance the width of the body, the sleeves are skinny. The long, graceful shoulder line is accented by an exposed seam.

## Finished measurements

52¾ (55¾, 58¾, 61½, 64½, 67½, 70¼)" [134(141.5, 149, 156, 164, 171.5, 178.5)cm] bust circumference; shown in size 55¾" [141.5 cm] on a 32" [81 cm], 5'10" [178 cm] tall model (23¾" [60.5 cm] positive ease)

## Yarn

Owl by Quince & Co

(50% American wool, 50% alpaca; 120yd [110m]/50g)

- 11 (12, 12, 13, 14, 15, 16) skeins Elf 303

## Needles

- One 32" circular needle (circ) in size US 9 [5.5 mm]
- One 32" circ in size US 8 [5 mm]
- One 24" circ in size US 7 [4.5 mm]
- One set double-pointed needles in size US 9 [5.5 mm]

Or size to obtain gauge

## Notions

- Stitch markers
- Waste yarn
- Tapestry needle

## Gauge

16½ sts and 25 rnds = 4" [10 cm] in reverse stockinette stitch with largest needles, after wet blocking

17 sts and 21 rnds = 4" [10 cm] in half brioche stitch with middle-sized needles, after wet blocking.

## Half brioche stitch (even number of stitches)

Rnd 1: *K1, sl1yo; rep from * to end.
Rnd 2: *K1, brp; rep from *.
Repeat Rnds 1 and 2 for half brioche stitch.

## Note

Pullover is worked in the round, from the bottom up to underarm. Front and back are worked flat to shoulders with short row shaping, then joined using the three-needle bind off. Stitches are picked up around armhole edge and worked in the round to cuff. Stitches are picked up around neck edge and worked in a rib trim.

Half brioche is a great variation on full brioche stitch. It's slightly more stable, and each side has a look distinct from the other. On one side, it has strong vertical lines of knitted stitches, on the other—the side used here—the stitches are rounded and soft.

In sweaters as minimal as this one, details make all the difference. Exposed shoulder seams, made by working a three-needle bind off with the wrong sides together, add interest.

# pullover

## Pocket lining (Make 2)

With largest circular needle (circ), or if you prefer, work back and forth on two double-pointed needles (dpns), using the long-tail cast on, CO 24 sts.

**First row:** (RS) Purl.

Cont in rev St st for 6" [15 cm], ending after a WS (knit) row.

**Next row:** (RS) BO 1 st, purl to end.

**Next row:** BO 1 st, knit to end—22 sts rem.

Break yarn. Place sts onto waste yarn.

## Body

With middle-sized circ and using the long-tail cast on, CO 218 (230, 242, 254, 266, 278, 290) sts. Place marker (pm) for beg of rnd (BOR) and join to work in the rnd, careful not to twist sts.

## Begin half brioche trim

**First rnd:** Work Rnd 1 of half brioche st to end.

Cont in patt for 6½" [16.5 cm], ending after Rnd 1. Change to largest circ.

## Begin reverse stockinette and join pocket linings

**Next rnd:** P109 (115, 121, 127, 133, 139, 145), pm for side, p17 (19, 21, 23, 25, 27, 29), BO next 22 sts in p1, k1 rib, p31 (33, 35, 37, 39, 41, 43), BO next 22 sts in p1, k1 rib, p17 (19, 21, 23, 25, 27, 29) sts to end (BOR marker counts as second side marker).

**Next rnd:** *Purl to BO sts, with RS (purl) facing, place sts for pocket lining onto LH needle, then purl across; rep from * one more time, purl to end.

**Next rnd:** Purl.

Cont in rev St st until pc meas 14" [35.5 cm] from beg.

## Begin side shaping

**Next rnd** *inc rnd:* *P1, m1-p, purl to 1 st before side marker (m), m1-p, p1; rep from * one more time (4 sts inc'd)—222 (234, 246, 258, 270, 282, 294) sts.

Rep *inc rnd* every 4 rnds one more time, then every 2 rnds two times—234 (246, 258, 270, 282, 294, 306) sts; 117 (123, 129, 135, 141, 147, 153) sts each for front and back.

## Separate front and back

**Next rnd:** Using the cable cast on, CO 5 sts, purl to m, then place rem sts for front onto waste yarn.

## Back

**Next row:** (WS) Using the backward loop cast on, CO 5 sts, then knit to end—127 (133, 139, 145, 151, 157, 163) sts.

**Next row:** Purl.

Cont in rev St st until pc meas 5¼ (5¾, 6¼, 6¾, 7¼, 7¾, 8¼)" [13.5 (14.5, 16, 17, 18.5, 19.5, 21) cm] from underarm, ending after a WS row.

**Next row** *place markers:* (RS) P52 (55, 57, 59, 61, 63, 65), pm for neck, p23 (23, 25, 27, 29, 31, 33), pm for neck, p52 (55, 57, 59, 61, 63, 65) sts to end.

## Begin shoulder shaping

Do not count yarnovers as stitches.

**Next row** *short row 1:* (WS) Knit to last 4 (5, 5, 5, 6, 6, 6) sts, turn; (RS) yo, purl to last 4 (5, 5, 5, 6, 6, 6) sts, turn.

**Next row** *short row 2:* (WS) Yo, knit to 4 (4, 4, 5, 5, 5, 6) sts before last gap, turn; (RS) yo, purl to 4 (4, 4, 5, 5, 5, 6) sts before last gap, turn.

**Next row** *short row 3:* Rep *short row 2.*

**Next row** *short row 4:* (WS) Yo, knit to 4 (5, 5, 5, 6, 6) sts before last gap, turn; (RS) yo, purl to 4 (5, 5, 5, 5, 6, 6) sts before last gap, turn.

**Next row** *short row 5:* Rep *short row 4.*

## Begin neck shaping

**Next row** *short row 6:* (WS) Yo, knit to 5 (5, 5, 6, 6, 6) sts before last gap, turn; (RS) yo, purl to m, remove m, join a new ball of yarn and BO all sts to next m, removing marker to BO last st, purl to 5 (5, 5, 5, 6, 6, 6) sts before last gap, turn—52 (55, 57, 59, 61, 63, 65) sts rem for each side.

**Next row** *short row 7:* (WS) Yo, knit to left neck edge; on right neck edge, BO 5 sts, knit to 5 (5, 6, 6, 6, 6, 6) sts before last gap, turn; (RS) yo, purl to neck edge; then BO 5 sts, purl to 5 (5, 6, 6, 6, 6, 6) sts before last gap, turn—47 (50, 52, 54, 56, 58, 60) sts rem each.

**Next row** *short row 8:* (WS) Yo, knit to neck edge; then BO 6 sts, knit to 5 (5, 6, 6, 6, 6, 6) sts before last gap, turn; (RS) yo, purl to neck edge; then BO 6 sts, purl to 5 (5, 6, 6, 6, 6, 6) sts before last gap, turn—41 (44, 46, 48, 50, 52, 54) sts rem each.

**Next row:** (WS) Yo, knit to neck edge; then knit to end, ssk each yo with the st after gap.

**Next row:** (RS) With yarn attached at left neck edge, purl to end, ssp each yo with the st after gap.

Break yarn at each armhole edge. Place sts onto waste yarn.

## Front

Return sts held for front to largest circ.

**Next row:** (RS) With RS of front facing and beg at left armhole edge, pick up and knit 5 sts in underarm CO from left back, purl across front sts, then pick up and knit 5 sts in underarm CO from right back—127 (133, 139, 145, 151, 157, 163) sts on needle.

**Next row:** Knit.

Cont in rev St st until pc meas 5¼ (5¾, 6¼, 6¾, 7¼, 7¾, 8¼)" [13.5 (14.5, 16, 17, 18.5, 19.5, 21) cm] from underarm, ending after a WS row.

**Next row** *place markers:* (RS) P58 (61, 63, 66, 67, 69, 71), pm for neck, p11 (11, 13, 13, 17, 19, 21), pm for neck, p58 (61, 63, 66, 67, 69, 71) sts to end.

## Begin shoulder and neck shaping

Do not count yarnovers as stitches.

**Next row** *short row 1:* (WS) Knit to last 4 (5, 5, 5, 6, 6, 6) sts, turn; (RS) yo, purl to m, remove m, join a new ball of yarn and BO all sts to next m, removing marker to BO last st, purl to last 4 (5, 5, 5, 6, 6, 6) sts, turn—58 (61, 63, 66, 67, 69, 71) sts rem for each side.

**Next row** *short row 2:* (WS) Yo, knit to right neck edge; on left neck edge, BO 4 sts, knit to 4 (4, 4, 5, 5, 5, 6) sts before last gap, turn; (RS) yo, purl to neck edge; then BO 4 sts, purl to 4 (4, 4, 5, 5, 5, 6) sts before last gap, turn—54 (57, 59, 62, 63, 65, 67) sts rem each.

**Next row** *short row 3:* (WS) Yo, knit to neck edge; then BO 3 sts, knit to 4 (4, 4, 5, 5, 5, 6) sts before last gap, turn; (RS) yo, purl to neck edge; then BO 3 sts, purl to 4 (4, 4, 5, 5, 5, 6) sts before last gap, turn—51 (54, 56, 59, 60, 62, 64) sts rem each.

**Next row** *short row 4:* (WS) Yo, knit to neck edge; then BO 3 sts, knit to 4 (5, 5, 5, 5, 6, 6) sts before last gap, turn; (RS) yo, purl to neck edge; then BO 3 sts, purl to 4 (5, 5, 5, 5, 6, 6) sts before last gap, turn—48 (51, 53, 56, 57, 59, 61) sts rem each.

**Next row** *short row 5:* (WS) Yo, knit to neck edge; then BO 2 sts, knit to 4 (5, 5, 5, 5, 6, 6) sts before last gap, turn; (RS) yo, purl to neck edge; then BO 2 sts, purl to 4 (5, 5, 5, 5, 6, 6) sts before last gap, turn—46 (49, 51, 54, 55, 57, 59) sts rem each.

**Next row** *short row 6:* (WS) Yo, knit to neck edge; then BO 2 sts, knit to 5 (5, 5, 5, 6, 6, 6) sts before last gap, turn; (RS) yo, purl to neck edge; then BO 2 sts, purl to 5 (5, 5, 5, 6, 6, 6) sts before last gap, turn—44 (47, 49, 52, 53, 55, 57) sts rem each.

**Next row** *short row 7:* (WS) Yo, knit to neck edge; then BO 2 sts, knit to 5 (5, 6, 6, 6, 6, 6) sts before last gap, turn; (RS) yo, purl to neck edge; then BO 2 sts, purl to 5 (5, 6, 6, 6, 6, 6) sts before last gap, turn—42 (45, 47, 50, 51, 53, 55) sts rem each.

**Next row** *short row 8:* (WS) Yo, knit to neck edge; then BO 1 st, knit to 5 (5, 6, 6, 6, 6, 6) sts before last gap, turn; (RS) yo, purl to neck edge; then BO 1, purl to 5 (5, 6, 6, 6, 6, 6) sts before last gap, turn—41 (44, 46, 49, 50, 52, 54) sts rem each.

**Next row:** (WS) Knit to neck edge; then knit to end, ssk each yo with the st after gap.

**Next row:** (RS) With yarn attached at right neck edge, purl to end, ssp each yo with the st after gap. Do not break yarn, leave sts on needle.

## Join shoulders

Place sts held for back shoulders onto smaller circ. With WS (knit) of pcs tog and yarn attached at armhole edge, using the three-needle bind off, BO all right shoulder sts. Rep for left shoulder.

Gently steam block piece.

## Sleeves

With RS facing and dpns, beg at underarm, pick up and knit 23 (25, 27, 29, 31, 33, 35) sts along armhole edge to shoulder seam (approx 2 sts for every 3 rows), then pick up and knit 23 (25, 27, 29, 31, 33, 35) sts to underarm—46 (50, 54, 58, 62, 66, 70) sts on needles. Pm for BOR.

**First rnd:** Purl.

**Next rnd:** Purl.

### Begin sleeve shaping

**Next rnd** *dec rnd:* P2, p2tog, purl to last 4 sts, p2tog, p2 (2 sts dec'd)—44 (48, 52, 56, 60, 64, 68) sts rem.

Rep *dec rnd* every 2 rnds 4 (4, 5, 5, 8, 8, 8) more times, every 4 rnds 3 (3, 4, 4, 4, 4, 4) times, then every 6 rnds 2 (2, 2, 2, 1, 1, 1) times—26 (30, 30, 34, 34, 38, 42) sts rem.

Work even in rev St st until sleeve meas 7" [18 cm] from pick-up.

### Begin cuff trim

**Next rnd:** Work Rnd 1 of half brioche st to end.

**Next rnd:** Work Rnd 2 of patt.

Cont in patt for 4" [10 cm], ending after Rnd 2.

**Next rnd:** Bind off in k1, p1 rib.

### Finishing

Weave in ends. Wet block pullover to finished measurements.

Sew pocket linings to WS of front.

## Neck trim

With RS facing and smallest circ, beg at right shoulder seam, pick up and knit 1 st in shoulder seam, pick up and knit 45 (45, 47, 49, 51, 53, 55) sts along back neck edge to left shoulder (1 st in each BO st), pm, pick up and knit 1 st in shoulder seam and 1 st in front side of neck edge, pick up and knit 45 (45, 47, 47, 51, 53, 55) sts along front neck (1 st in each BO st), then pick up and knit 1 st in front side of neck edge— 94 (94, 98, 100, 106, 110, 114) sts on needle. Pm for BOR.

## Begin rib

**Rnd 1:** *P1, k1; rep from * to end.
**Rnd 2** *dec rnd:* *Work in rib to 2 sts before m, sl 2 sts tog knitwise, remove m, k1, pass the 2 sl sts over, replace m; rep from * one more time (4 sts dec'd)—90 (90, 94, 96, 102, 106, 110) sts rem.
**Rnd 3:** *(K1, p1) to 2 sts before m, k2; rep from * one more time.
**Rnd 4:** Rep *dec rnd*—86 (86, 90, 92, 98, 102, 106) sts rem.

Rep Rnds 1-4 one more time—78 (78, 82, 84, 90, 94, 98) sts rem.
**Next rnd:** Work in rib as est.
**Next rnd:** Bind off as follows: K1, then *BO in patt to 2 sts before m, sl 2 sts tog knitwise, remove m, k1, pass the 2 sl sts over, then BO this st; rep from * one more time.

Weave in rem ends and block again, if you like.

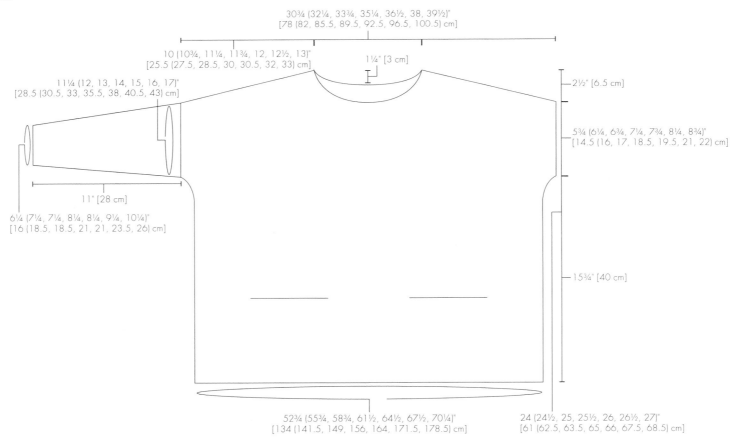

30¾ (32¼, 33¾, 35¼, 36½, 38, 39½)"
[78 (82, 85.5, 89.5, 92.5, 96.5, 100.5) cm]

10 (10¾, 11¼, 11¾, 12, 12½, 13)"
[25.5 (27.5, 28.5, 30, 30.5, 32, 33) cm]

1¼" [3 cm]

11¼ (12, 13, 14, 15, 16, 17)"
[28.5 (30.5, 33, 35.5, 38, 40.5, 43) cm]

2½" [6.5 cm]

5¾ (6¼, 6¾, 7¼, 7¾, 8¼, 8¾)"
[14.5 (16, 17, 18.5, 19.5, 21, 22) cm]

11" [28 cm]

6¼ (7¼, 7¼, 8¼, 8¼, 9¼, 10¼)"
[16 (18.5, 18.5, 21, 21, 23.5, 26) cm]

15¾" [40 cm]

52¾ (55¾, 58¾, 61½, 64½, 67½, 70¼)"
[134 (141.5, 149, 156, 164, 171.5, 178.5) cm]

24 (24½, 25, 25½, 26, 26½, 27)"
[61 (62.5, 63.5, 65, 66, 67.5, 68.5) cm]

# chestnut

Crossing stitches to create a cable pattern is a technique that can yield all kinds of vertical panel patterns. But the simple technique of knitting stitches out of order can be used in an all-over pattern, too, as it is here in this open cardigan. Chestnut is worked completely in the stitch pattern. The pattern lies flat, so no need for borders at sweater bottom or cuffs. The only thing added is the deep ribbed band which finishes the center front edges and forms a collar around the neck.

## Finished measurements
34¾ (42¼, 50, 57½, 65)" [88.5 (107.5, 127, 146, 165) cm] bust circumference; shown in size 42¼" [107.5 cm] on a 32" [81.5 cm], 5'10" [178 cm] tall model (10¼" [26 cm] positive ease)

## Yarn
Owl by Quince & Co
(50% American wool, 50% alpaca; 120yd [110m]/50g)
• 8 (10, 11, 13, 15) skeins Tawny 302

## Needles
• One 32" circular needle (circ) in size US 10 [6 mm]
• One 32" circ in size US 7 [4.5 mm]
• One set double-pointed needles in size US 10 [6 mm]

## Or size to obtain gauge

## Notions
• Stitch markers
• Cable needle
• Waste yarn
• Tapestry needle

## Gauge
17 sts and 20 rows = 4" [10 cm] in cable pattern with larger needles, after wet blocking.

## Special abbreviations
C4B (cable 4 back, leans to the right): Slip 2 stitches onto cable needle (cn) and hold in back, k2, then k2 from cn.
C4F (cable 4 front, leans to the left): Slip 2 stitches onto cn and hold in front, k2, then k2 from cn.

## Cable pattern (multiple of 8 sts)
*Worked flat*
Row 1: (RS) Knit.
Row 2 and all WS rows: Purl.
Row 3: *C4B, k4; rep from * to end.
Row 5: Knit.
Row 7: *K4, C4F; rep from * to end.
Row 8: (WS) Purl.
Repeat Rows 1-8 for cable pattern.

*In the round*
Work odd-numbered rounds same as for working flat. On even-numbered rounds, knit.

## Note
Cardi is worked flat from the bottom up, in one piece to underarm, then fronts and back are worked separately to shoulder, and joined using the three-needle bind off. Stitches are picked up around armhole edge and worked in the round to cuff. Stitches are picked up along fronts and back neck and worked in a rib trim.

---

Chestnut is shaped along the sides, meaning it's wider at the hem than at the underarm. But working decreases in a repeating stitch pattern can be tricky. Suddenly, instead of the eight stitches needed for the repeat, there are seven. By avoiding shaping in pattern at the sides (decreases are worked in a stockinette side panel), Chestnut allows you plenty of time to get acquainted with the cables before decreasing in pattern for the sleeves.

Make this sweater an easy knit by working the cable pattern without a cable needle. Visit our blog for instructions.

# cardi

With larger circular needle (circ) and using the long-tail cast on, CO 138 (170, 202, 234, 266) sts. Do not join.

## Begin stitch pattern

**First row:** (RS) K1, work Row 1 of cable pattern to last st, k1.

**Next row:** P1, work next row of patt to last st, p1. Work 15 more rows as est.

**Next row** *place markers:* (WS) P25 (33, 41, 49, 57), place marker for side (pm), p8, pm for side, p72 (88, 104, 120, 136), pm for side, p8, pm for side, p25 (33, 41, 49, 57) sts to end.

## Begin side shaping

**Next row** *dec row:* (RS) K1, *work in patt to marker (m), slip marker (sl m), ssk, knit to 2 sts before next m, k2tog; rep from * one more time, work in patt to last st, k1 (4 sts dec'd)—134 (166, 198, 230, 262) sts rem.

Rep *dec row* every 18 rows two more times—126 (158, 190, 222, 254) sts rem.

Work 19 rows even, ending after a WS row. Piece meas approx 14½" [37 cm] from beg. Make note of last row worked in pattern.

## Separate fronts and back

**Next row:** (RS) Removing markers as you go, work as est to first m, k1, place next 74 (90, 106, 122, 138) sts onto waste yarn for back, then place rem 26 (34, 42, 50, 58) sts onto separate waste yarn for left front—26 (34, 42, 50, 58) sts rem on needle for right front.

## Right front

**Next row:** (WS) Using the cable cast on, CO 8 sts, purl to end, removing marker—34 (42, 50, 58, 66) sts.

**Next row:** (RS) K1, work in patt to last st, k1.

**Next row:** Purl.

Cont in patt until pc meas 6 (7, 8, 9, 10)" [15 (18, 20.5, 23, 25.5) cm] from underarm, ending after a WS row.

Break yarn. Place sts onto waste yarn.

## Left front

Return sts held for left front to larger circ. Join yarn ready to work a RS row.

**Next row:** (RS) Using the cable cast on, CO 8 sts, work next row of patt to last st, k1—34 (42, 50, 58, 66) sts.

**Next row:** Purl.

**Next row:** K1, work in patt to last st, k1.

Cont in patt until left front meas same as right front, ending after the same WS row.

Break yarn leaving a long tail for finishing. Place sts onto waste yarn.

## Back

Return rem sts held for back to larger circ.

**Next row:** (RS) With RS of back facing and beg at right armhole edge, pick up and knit 8 sts in underarm CO from right front, work next row of patt across back sts, then pick up and knit 8 sts in underarm CO from left front—90 (106, 122, 138, 154) sts on needle.

**Next row:** Purl.

**Next row:** (RS) K1, work in patt to last st, k1.

Cont in patt until back meas same as fronts, ending after the same WS row.

Do not break yarn.

## Join shoulders

Place sts held for left and right front onto smaller circ. With RS of pcs tog and attached yarn, using the three-needle bind off, BO all sts for right front with corresponding back sts. With long tail at left armhole edge, rep for left shoulder, then BO rem 22 sts for back neck.

Gently steam block piece.

## Sleeves

With RS facing and double-pointed needles, beg at underarm, pick up and knit 25 (29, 33, 37, 41) sts to shoulder seam (approx 4 sts for every 5 rows), then pick up and knit 25 (29, 33, 37, 41) sts to underarm—50 (58, 66, 74, 82) sts on needles. Pm for beg of rnd.

**First rnd:** Knit.

## Begin cable pattern
**Next rnd:** K1, work Rnd 1 of cable patt to last st, k1.
Cont as est until Rnds 1-8 of patt have been worked, then work Rnd 1 one more time.

## Begin sleeve shaping
*Note:* Decreases occur on knit rnds. On cable rounds, maintain cable pattern when possible. When there are not enough stitches at beginning or end of round to complete a cable, work these stitches in stockinette.

**Next rnd** *dec rnd:* K1, k2tog, knit to last 3 sts, ssk, k1 (2 sts dec'd)—48 (56, 64, 72, 80) sts rem.
Cont in patt and rep *dec rnd* every 8 (6, 4, 4, 2) rnds 1 (3, 3, 11, 1) more times, then every 10 (8, 6, 6, 4) rnds 4 (4, 7, 2, 14) times—38 (42, 44, 46, 50) sts rem.
Work even in patt until sleeve meas approx 14¾" [37.5 cm] from pick-up, ending after Rnd 4 or 8 of patt.
**Next rnd:** Bind off knitwise.

## Finishing
Weave in ends. Wet block cardi to finished measurements.

## Neck trim
With RS facing and smaller circ, beg at lower edge of right front, pick up and knit 88 (92, 96, 100, 104) sts to shoulder seam (approx 4 sts for every 5 rows), pick up and knit 22 sts along back neck (1 st in each BO st), then pick up and knit 88 (92, 96, 100, 104) sts along left front to end—198 (206, 214, 222, 230) sts on needle.

## Begin rib
**First row:** (WS) *P2, k2; rep from * to last 2 sts, p2.
**Next row:** *K2, p2; rep from * to last 2 sts, k2.
Cont in rib for 2½" [6.5 cm], ending after a WS row.
**Next row:** (RS) Bind off in pattern.

Weave in rem ends. Block again, if you like.

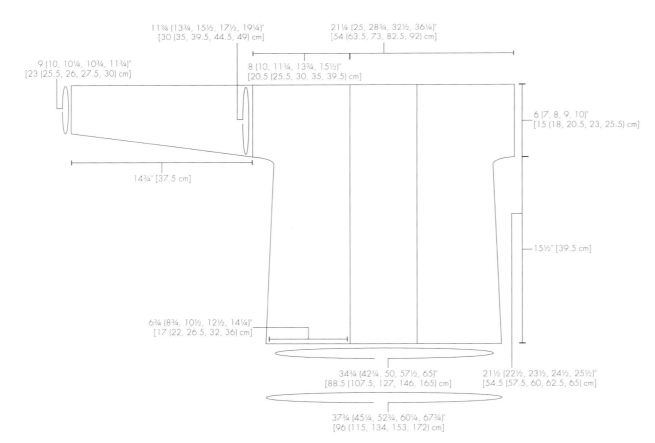

11¾ (13¾, 15½, 17½, 19¼)"
[30 (35, 39.5, 44.5, 49) cm]

21¼ (25, 28¾, 32½, 36¼)"
[54 (63.5, 73, 82.5, 92) cm]

9 (10, 10¼, 10¾, 11¾)"
[23 (25.5, 26, 27.5, 30) cm]

8 (10, 11¾, 13¾, 15½)"
[20.5 (25.5, 30, 35, 39.5) cm]

6 (7, 8, 9, 10)"
[15 (18, 20.5, 23, 25.5) cm]

14¾" [37.5 cm]

15½" [39.5 cm]

6¾ (8¾, 10½, 12½, 14¼)"
[17 (22, 26.5, 32, 36) cm]

34¾ (42¼, 50, 57½, 65)"
[88.5 (107.5, 127, 146, 165) cm]

21½ (22½, 23½, 24½, 25½)"
[54.5 (57.5, 60, 62.5, 65) cm]

37¾ (45¼, 53¾, 60¼, 67¾)"
[96 (115, 134, 153, 172) cm]

# birch

Deep, round, patterned-yoke pullovers originated in Iceland. But these lovely sweaters are now part of all knitters' lexicons. Birch is an oversized version, roomy and warm, striking in only two colors. And it's a hybrid structure. The body of the sweater is knitted from the bottom up, but the sleeves are knitted from the yoke down, so you can adjust length as you go.

## Finished measurements

32 (38½, 44¼, 50¾, 56½, 62, 68¾)" [81.5 (98, 112.5, 129, 143.5, 157.5, 174.5)cm] bust circumference; shown in size 44¼" [112.5 cm] on a 32" [81.5 cm], 5'10" [178 cm] tall model (12½" [32 cm] positive ease)

## Yarn

### Owl by Quince & Co

(50% American wool, 50% alpaca; 120yd [110m]/50g)

- 7 (8, 9, 10, 11, 12, 14) skeins Togian 333 (MC)
- 2 (2, 2, 2, 3, 3, 3) skeins Snowy 300 (CC)

## Needles

- One 32" circular needle (circ) in size US 9 [5.5 mm]
- One 16" circ in size US 9 [5.5 mm]
- One 32" circ in size US 8 [5 mm]
- One 16" circ in size US 8 [5 mm]
- One set double-pointed needles (dpns) in size US 9 [5.5 mm]
- One set dpns in size US 8 [5 mm]

### Or size to obtain gauge

## Notions

- Stitch markers
- Waste yarn
- Tapestry needle

## Gauge

17 sts and 24 rnds = 4" [10 cm] in stockinette stitch with larger needles, after wet blocking.

## Notes

1. Body is knitted in the round from the bottom up to underarm. Stitches are held for underarm, then cast on to waste yarn to later become the sleeves. Yoke is continued in a colorwork pattern with round yoke shaping to neck edge. Stitches are picked up from waste yarn and worked in the round to cuff.

2. When picking up live stitches from the bottom edge of a cast on, you will have one more stitch than the number you cast on. See page 109 for an illustrated tutorial.

# pullover

With MC and smaller, longer circular needle (circ), using the long-tail cast on, CO 136 (164, 188, 216, 240, 264, 292) sts. Place marker (pm) for beg of rnd (BOR) and join to work in the rnd, careful not to twist sts.

## Begin rib trim
First rnd: *K2, p2; rep from * to end.
Cont in rib for 2¼" [5.5 cm].
Change to larger, longer circ.
Next rnd place marker: K68 (82, 94, 108, 120, 132, 146), pm for side, k68 (82, 94, 108, 120, 132, 146) sts to end (BOR counts as second side marker).

## Begin stockinette
Next rnd: Knit.
Cont in St st until pc meas 15" [38 cm] from beg.
Next rnd: *Knit to side m, remove m, k3 (4, 4, 5, 5, 5, 6), then place last 6 (8, 8, 10, 10, 10, 12) sts onto waste yarn; rep from * one more time— 62 (74, 86, 98, 110, 122, 134) sts rem each for front and back.

## Begin yoke
Next rnd inc rnd: K31 (37, 43, 49, 55, 61, 67), pm for new BOR, m1, k31 (37, 43, 49, 55, 61, 67), turn work, with waste yarn, make a slipknot (first sleeve st), place on RH needle and using the backward loop cast on, CO 49 (53, 57, 61, 65, 69, 73) more sts for sleeve, turn work, with MC, knit sts cast on for sleeve, k31 (37, 43, 49, 55, 61, 67), m1, k31 (37, 43, 49, 55, 61, 67), turn work, with waste yarn, make a slipknot (first sleeve st), place on RH needle and using the backward loop cast on,

CO 49 (53, 57, 61, 65, 69, 73) more sts for sleeve, turn work, with MC, knit sts cast on for sleeve, k31 (37, 43, 49, 55, 61, 67) sts to end (2 sts inc'd)—224 (256, 288, 320, 352, 384, 416) sts on needle.
First rnd: Knit.
Knit 0 (1, 2, 6, 10, 14, 18) more rnds.

## Begin chart A
See also chart, page 71.
Next rnd: Work Rnd 1 of chart A to end.
Cont in patt until Rnds 1-11 have been worked.

### Sizes 32 (38½, 44¼, -, -, 62, -)" [81.5 (98, 112.5, -, -, 157.5, -) cm] only:
Proceed to All sizes.

### Sizes - (-, -, 50¾, 56½, -, 68¾)" [- (-, -, 129, 143.5, -, 174.5) cm] only:
Next rnd dec rnd: With MC, *k-(-, -, 8, 20, -, 11), k2tog; rep from * to end; - (-, -, 32, 16, -, 32) sts dec'd— - (-, -, 288, 336, -, 384) sts rem.

## All sizes
With MC, knit 1 (2, 3, 2, 2, 3, 2) rnds.
Next rnd dec rnd: *K26 (14, 4, 4, 5, 2, 2), k2tog; rep from * to end; 8 (16, 48, 48, 48, 96, 96) sts dec'd—216 (240, 240, 240, 288, 288, 288) sts rem.

## Begin chart B
See also chart, page 71.
Next rnd: Work Rnd 1 of chart B to end.
Cont in patt until Rnds 1-15 have been worked.
Next rnd: With MC, knit.
Next rnd dec rnd: *K1, (k2tog) 1 (2, 2, 2, 1, 1, 1) times; rep from * to end; 72 (96, 96, 96, 96, 96, 96) sts dec'd—144 (144, 144, 144, 192, 192, 192) sts rem.
Knit 1 (2, 3, 3, 3, 3, 3) rnds.

## Begin chart C
See also chart, page 71.
Next rnd: Work Rnd 1 of chart C to end.
Cont in patt until Rnds 1-6 have been worked.
With MC, knit 1 (2, 3, 3, 3, 3, 3) rnds.
Change to shorter, larger circ.
Next rnd dec rnd: *K1 (1, 1, 1, 0, 0, 0), k2tog; rep from * to end; 48 (48, 48, 48, 96, 96, 96) sts dec'd—96 sts rem.

## Begin chart D
See also chart, page 71.
Next rnd: Work Rnd 1 of chart D to end.
Cont in patt until Rnds 1-3 have been worked.
Break CC.
Next rnd dec rnd: With MC, *k4, k2tog; rep from * to end (16 sts dec'd)—80 sts rem.
Change to smaller, shorter circ.

## Begin neck trim
Next rnd: P1, *k2, p2; rep from *, end k2, p1.
Cont in rib for 1¼" [3 cm].
Next rnd: Bind off in pattern.

## Sleeves

With MC, RS facing, and larger double-pointed needles (dpns), place first 3 (4, 4, 5, 5, 5, 6) sts held for underarm onto needle, pm for BOR, place rem 3 (4, 4, 5, 5, 5, 6) underarm sts onto needle, then, working one st at a time, pick out waste yarn from sleeve cast on and place each st onto needle—56 (62, 66, 72, 76, 80, 86) sts on needles.

## Begin sleeve shaping

**First rnd** *dec rnd:* K3, k2tog, knit to last 5 sts, ssk, k3 (2 sts dec'd)—54 (60, 64, 70, 74, 78, 84) sts rem.

Rep *dec rnd* every 10 (8, 8, 6, 6, 4, 4) rnds 6 (4, 4, 7, 7, 1, 10) more times, then every 12 (10, 10, 8, 8, 6, 6) rnds 1 (4, 4, 4, 4, 12, 6) times—40 (44, 48, 48, 52, 52, 52) sts rem. Work even in St st until sleeve meas 14" [35.5 cm] from underarm.

## Begin chart D

**Next rnd:** Work Rnd 1 of chart D to end. Cont in patt until Rnds 1-3 have been worked. Break CC.
With MC, knit 1 rnd.
Change to smaller dpns.

## Begin cuff trim

**Next rnd:** P1, *k2, p2; rep from *, end k2, p1.
Cont in rib for 1½" [5 cm].
**Next rnd:** Bind off in pattern.

## Finishing

Weave in ends. Wet block pullover to finished measurements.

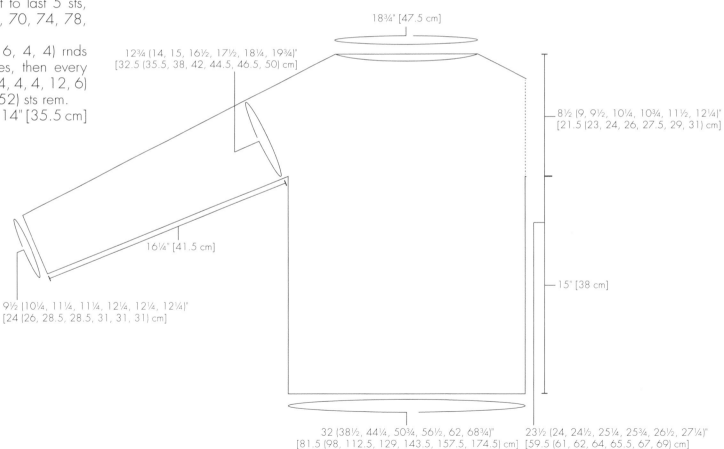

18¾" [47.5 cm]

12¾ (14, 15, 16½, 17½, 18¼, 19¾)"
[32.5 (35.5, 38, 42, 44.5, 46.5, 50) cm]

8½ (9, 9½, 10¼, 10¾, 11½, 12¼)"
[21.5 (23, 24, 26, 27.5, 29, 31) cm]

16¼" [41.5 cm]

9½ (10¼, 11¼, 11¼, 12¼, 12¼, 12¼)"
[24 (26, 28.5, 28.5, 31, 31, 31) cm]

15" [38 cm]

32 (38½, 44¼, 50¾, 56½, 62, 68¾)"
[81.5 (98, 112.5, 129, 143.5, 157.5, 174.5) cm]

23½ (24, 24½, 25¼, 25¾, 26½, 27¼)"
[59.5 (61, 62, 64, 65.5, 67, 69) cm]

## Chart A

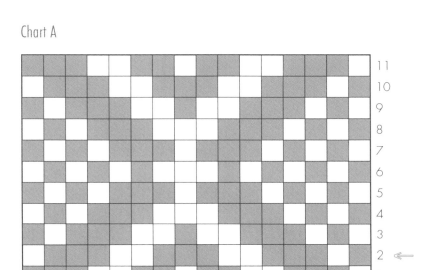

11
10
9
8
7
6
5
4
3
2
1

16 15 14 13 12 11 10 9 8 7 6 5 4 3 2 1

## Chart B

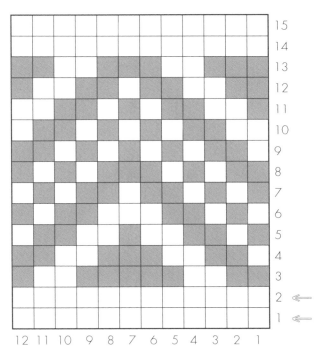

15
14
13
12
11
10
9
8
7
6
5
4
3
2
1

12 11 10 9 8 7 6 5 4 3 2 1

## Chart C

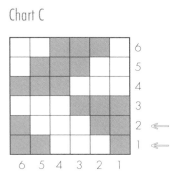

6
5
4
3
2
1

6 5 4 3 2 1

## Chart D

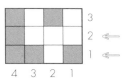

3
2
1

4 3 2 1

## Key

with MC, knit

with CC, knit

# oak

When you have a pretty yarn, sometimes you just want the sweater you're making to quietly send the yarn forward, the silhouette of the sweater taking a back seat. No cables or other stitch patterns, no buttons, no ornament—save a single pocket—distract from the warmth and texture of the yarn itself.

## Finished measurements
36½ (40¼, 44, 47½, 51¼, 54¾, 58½, 62¼)" [92.5 (102, 112, 120.5, 130, 139, 148.5, 158) cm] bust circumference; shown in size 40¼" [102 cm] on a 32" [81.5 cm], 5'10" [178 cm] tall model (8¼" [21 cm] positive ease)

## Yarn
### Owl by Quince & Co
(50% American wool, 50% alpaca; 120yd [110m]/50g)
- 8 (8, 9, 10, 10, 11, 12, 13) skeins Papuan 305

## Needles
- One 32" circular needle (circ) in size US 8 [5 mm]
- One 32" circ in size US 7 [4.5 mm]
- One 16" circ in size US 7 [4.5 mm]
- One set double-pointed needles (dpns) in size US 8 [5 mm]
- One set dpns in size US 7 [4.5 mm]

Or size to obtain gauge

## Notions
- Stitch markers
- Waste yarn
- Tapestry needle

## Gauge
17½ sts and 26 rnds = 4" [10 cm] in reverse stockinette stitch with larger needles, after wet blocking.

## Note
Pullover is worked in the round, from the bottom up to underarm, then front and back are worked flat to shoulders with short row shaping, and joined using the three-needle bind off. Stitches are picked up around armhole edge and worked in the round to cuff. Stitches are picked up around neck edge and worked in a rib trim.

# pullover

## Pocket lining (Make 1)
With larger circular needle (circ), or if you prefer, work back and forth on two double-pointed needles (dpns), using the long-tail cast on, CO 21 sts.
**First row:** (RS) Purl.
Cont in rev St st for 5" [12.5 cm], ending after a WS (knit) row.
**Next row:** (RS) BO 1 st, purl to end.
**Next row:** BO 1 st, knit to end—19 sts rem.
Break yarn. Place sts onto waste yarn.

## Body
With smaller, longer circ and using the long-tail cast on, CO 160 (176, 192, 208, 224, 240, 256, 272) sts. Place marker (pm) for beg of rnd (BOR) and join to work in the rnd, careful not to twist sts.

## Begin rib trim
**First rnd:** *K1, p1; rep from * to end.
Cont in rib for 1½" [4 cm].
Change to larger circ.

## Begin reverse stockinette
**Next rnd:** Purl.
Cont in rev St st until pc meas 6¼" [16.5 cm] from beg.
**Next rnd** *place markers:* Purl to last 25 (28, 30, 33, 35, 38, 40, 43) sts, pm for pocket, p19, pm for pocket, p6 (9, 11, 14, 16, 19, 21, 24) sts to end.

## Begin pocket trim

**Next rnd:** Purl to pocket marker (m), p1, *k1, p1; rep from * to next pocket m, purl to end.

Cont in rev St st and rib as est for 3 more rnds.

**Next rnd:** Purl to pocket m, remove m, BO all sts in patt to next pocket m, removing marker to BO last st, purl to end.

## Join pocket lining

**Next rnd:** Purl to BO sts, with RS (purl) facing, place sts for pocket lining onto LH needle and purl across, then purl to end—160 (176, 192, 208, 224, 240, 256, 272) sts on needle.

**Next rnd:** Purl.

Cont in rev St st until pc meas 11" [28 cm] from beg.

**Next rnd** *place marker:* P80 (88, 96, 104, 112, 120, 128, 136), pm for side, p80 (88, 96, 104, 112, 120, 128, 136) sts to end (BOR counts as second side marker).

## Begin side shaping

**Next rnd** *inc rnd:* *P1, m1-p, purl to 1 st before side m, m1-p, p1; rep from * one more time (4 sts inc'd)—164 (180, 196, 212, 228, 244, 260, 276) sts.

Rep *inc rnd* every 4 rnds one more time, then every 2 rnds two times—176 (192, 208, 224, 240, 256, 272, 288) sts; 88 (96, 104, 112, 120, 128, 136, 144) sts each for front and back.

## Separate front and back

**Next rnd:** Using the cable cast on, CO 6 sts, purl to side m, then place rem sts for front onto waste yarn.

## Back

**Next row:** (WS) Using the cable cast on, CO 6 sts, knit to end—100 (108, 116, 124, 132, 140, 148, 156) sts on needle.

**Next row:** Purl.

Cont in rev St st until pc meas 4½ (4¾, 5, 5½, 6, 6½, 7, 7½)" [11.5 (12, 12.5, 14, 15, 16.5, 18, 19) cm] from underarm, ending after a WS row.

**Next row** *place markers:* (RS) P33 (37, 41, 45, 47, 51, 55, 59), pm for neck, p34 (34, 34, 34, 38, 38, 38, 38), pm for neck, p33 (37, 41, 45, 47, 51, 55, 59) sts to end.

## Begin shoulder shaping

Do not count yarnovers as stitches.

**Next row** *short row 1:* (WS) Knit to last 5 (5, 6, 6, 6, 6, 7, 7) sts, turn; (RS) yo, purl to last 5 (5, 6, 6, 6, 6, 7, 7) sts, turn.

**Next row** *short row 2:* (WS) Yo, knit to 3 (4, 4, 5, 5, 6, 6, 7) sts before last gap, turn; (RS) yo, purl to 3 (4, 4, 5, 5, 6, 6, 7) sts before last gap, turn.

Rep *short row 2* five more times.

**Next row** *short row 3:* (WS) Yo, knit to 4 (4, 5, 5, 5, 5, 6, 6) sts before last gap, turn; (RS) yo, purl to m, remove m, join a new ball of yarn and BO all sts to next m, removing marker to BO last st, purl to 4 (4, 5, 5, 5, 5, 6, 6) sts before last gap, turn—33 (37, 41, 45, 47, 51, 55, 59) sts rem for each side.

**Next row:** (WS) Yo, knit to neck edge; then knit to end, ssk each yo with the st after gap.

**Next row:** Purl to neck edge; then purl to end, ssp each yo with the st after gap.

Break yarn leaving a long tail at armhole edge for finishing. Place sts onto waste yarn.

## Front

Return sts held for front to larger circ.

**Next row:** (RS) With RS of front facing and beg at left armhole edge, pick up and knit 6 sts in underarm CO from left back, purl across front sts, then pick up and knit 6 sts in underarm CO from right back—100 (108, 116, 124, 132, 140, 148, 156) sts on needle.

**Next row:** Knit.

Cont in rev St st until pc meas 4½ (4¾, 5, 5½, 6, 6½, 7, 7½)" [11.5 (12, 12.5, 14, 15, 16.5, 18, 19) cm] from underarm, ending after a WS row.

**Next row** *place markers:* (RS) P41 (45, 49, 53, 55, 59, 63, 67), pm for neck, p18 (18, 18, 18, 22, 22, 22, 22), pm for neck, p41 (45, 49, 53, 55, 59, 63, 67) sts to end.

## Begin shoulder shaping

Do not count yarnovers as stitches.

**Next row** *short row 1:* (WS) Knit to last 5 (5, 6, 6, 6, 7, 7) sts, turn; (RS) yo, purl to last 5 (5, 6, 6, 6, 6, 7, 7) sts, turn.

## Begin neck shaping

**Next row** *short row 2:* (WS) Yo, knit to last 3 (4, 4, 5, 5, 6, 6, 7) sts, turn; (RS) yo, purl to m, remove m, join a new ball of yarn and BO all sts to next m, removing marker to BO last st, purl to last 3 (4, 4, 5, 5, 6, 6, 7) sts, turn—41 (45, 49, 53, 55, 59, 63, 67) sts rem for each side.

**Next row** *short row 3:* (WS) Yo, knit to right neck edge; on left neck edge, BO 3 sts, knit to 3 (4, 4, 5, 5, 6, 6, 7) sts before last gap, turn; (RS) yo, purl to neck edge; then BO 3 sts, purl to 3 (4, 4, 5, 5, 6, 6, 7) sts before last gap, turn—38 (42, 46, 50, 52, 56, 60, 64) sts rem each.

**Next row** *short row 4:* (WS) Yo, knit to 2 sts before neck edge, k2tog; then ssk, knit to 3 (4, 4, 5, 5, 6, 6, 7) sts before last gap, turn; (RS) yo, purl to neck edge; then purl to 3 (4, 4, 5, 5, 6, 6, 7) sts before last gap, turn (2 sts dec'd)—37 (41, 45, 49, 51, 55, 59, 63) sts rem each.
Rep *short row four* 3 (4, 3, 4, 4, 3, 3, 3) more times—34 (37, 42, 45, 47, 52, 56, 60) sts rem each.

## Sizes - (40¼, -, 47½, 51¼, -, -, -)" [- (102, -, 120.5, 130, -, -, -) cm] only:
Proceed to All sizes.

## Sizes 36½ (-, 44, -, -, 54¾, 58½, 62¼)" [92.5 (-, 112, -, -, 139, 148.5, 158) cm] only:
**Next row** *short row 5:* (WS) Yo, knit to 2 sts before neck edge, k2tog; then ssk, knit to 4 (-, 5, -, -, 5, 6, 6) sts before last gap, turn; (RS) yo, purl to neck edge; then purl to 4 (-, 5, -, -, 5, 6, 6) sts before last gap, turn (2 sts dec'd)—33 (-, 41, -, -, 51, 55, 59) sts rem each.

## All sizes
**Next row:** (WS) Yo, knit to neck edge; then knit to end, ssk each yo with the st after gap.
**Next row:** Purl to neck edge; then, purl to end, ssp each yo with the st after gap.

## Join shoulders
Place sts held for back shoulders onto smaller circ. With WS (knit) of pcs tog and yarn attached at right armhole edge, using the three-needle bind off, BO all right shoulder sts. With long tail at left armhole edge, rep for left shoulder.

Gently steam block piece.

## Sleeves
With RS facing and larger dpns, beg at underarm, pick up and knit 25 (27, 28, 30, 33, 35, 38, 40) sts along armhole edge to shoulder seam (approx 3 sts for every 4 rows), then pick up and knit 25 (27, 28, 30, 33, 35, 38, 40) sts to underarm—50 (54, 56, 60, 66, 70, 76, 80) sts on needles. Pm for BOR.
**First rnd:** Purl.
Purl 7 more rnds.

## Begin sleeve shaping
**Next rnd** *dec rnd:* P2, p2tog, purl to last 4 sts, p2tog, p2 (2 sts dec'd)—48 (52, 54, 58, 64, 68, 74, 78) sts rem.
Rep *dec rnd* every 16 (10, 8, 8, 6, 4, 4, 4) rnds 3 (3, 2, 7, 7, 3, 9, 15) more times, then every 18 (12, 10, 10, 8, 6, 6, 6) rnds 1 (3, 5, 1, 3, 9, 5, 1) times—40 (40, 40, 42, 44, 44, 46, 46) sts rem.
Cont in rev St st until sleeve meas 12" [30.5 cm] from pick-up.
Change to smaller dpns.

## Begin cuff trim
**First rnd:** *K1, p1; rep from * to end.
Cont in rib for 5" [12.5 cm].
**Next rnd:** Bind off in pattern.

## Finishing
Weave in ends. Wet block pullover to finished measurements.
Sew pocket lining to WS of front.

## Neck trim
With RS facing and smaller, shorter circ, beg at right shoulder seam, pick up and knit 1 st in each BO st and 1 st in each row around neck edge, making sure to pick up an even number of sts. Pm for BOR.

## Begin rib
**First rnd:** *P1, k1; rep from * to end.
Cont in rib for 1" [2.5 cm].
**Next rnd:** Bind off in pattern.

Weave in rem ends and block again, if you like.

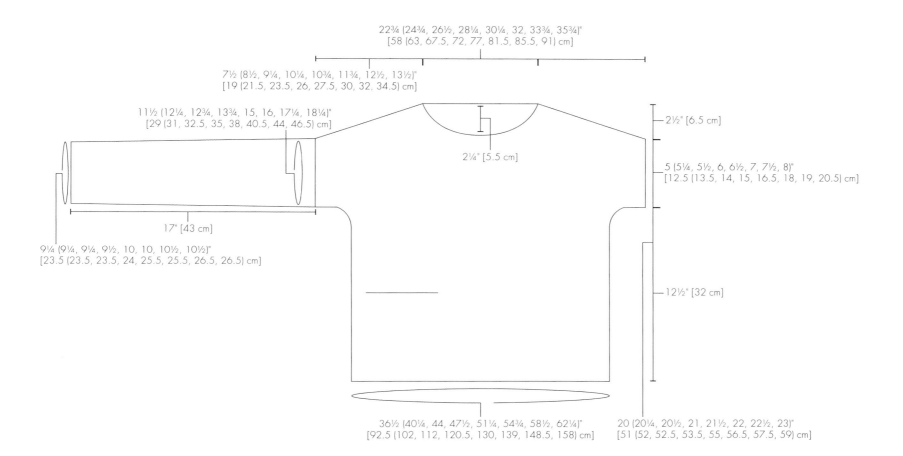

22¾ (24¾, 26½, 28¼, 30¼, 32, 33¾, 35¾)"
[58 (63, 67.5, 72, 77, 81.5, 85.5, 91) cm]

7½ (8½, 9¼, 10¼, 10¾, 11¾, 12½, 13½)"
[19 (21.5, 23.5, 26, 27.5, 30, 32, 34.5) cm]

11½ (12¼, 12¾, 13¾, 15, 16, 17¼, 18¼)"
[29 (31, 32.5, 35, 38, 40.5, 44, 46.5) cm]

2¼" [5.5 cm]

2½" [6.5 cm]

5 (5¼, 5½, 6, 6½, 7, 7½, 8)"
[12.5 (13.5, 14, 15, 16.5, 18, 19, 20.5) cm]

17" [43 cm]

9¼ (9¼, 9¼, 9½, 10, 10, 10½, 10½)"
[23.5 (23.5, 23.5, 24, 25.5, 25.5, 26.5, 26.5) cm]

12½" [32 cm]

36½ (40¼, 44, 47½, 51¼, 54¾, 58½, 62¼)"
[92.5 (102, 112, 120.5, 130, 139, 148.5, 158) cm]

20 (20¼, 20½, 21, 21½, 22, 22½, 23)"
[51 (52, 52.5, 53.5, 55, 56.5, 57.5, 59) cm]

# willow

Short columns of classic gansey knit-purl decorate the yoke on this otherwise plain sweater. And similar patterns on the tops of the sleeve extend the decorative element. The ribbed borders on body and cuff alternate columns of knit with columns of garter stitch, the latter serving to spread out the rib and prevent it from drawing in too much.

## Finished measurements

36½ (42½, 48½, 54½, 60½, 66½, 72½)" [92.5 (108, 123, 138.5, 153.5, 169, 184) cm] bust circumference; shown in size 48½" [123 cm] on a 32" [81.5 cm], 5'10" [178 cm] tall model (16½" [42 cm] positive ease)

## Yarn

### Owl by Quince & Co

(50% American wool, 50% alpaca; 120yd [110m]/50g)
- 7 (8, 10, 11, 13, 14, 16) skeins Buru 310

## Needles

- One 32" circular needle (circ) in size US 7 [4.5 mm]
- One 32" circ in size US 6 [4 mm]
- One 16" circ in size US 6 [4 mm]
- One set double-pointed needles (dpns) in size US 7 [4.5 mm]
- One set dpns in size US 6 [4 mm]

Or size to obtain gauge

## Notions

- Stitch markers
- Waste yarn
- Cable needle
- Tapestry needle

## Gauge

16 sts and 24 rnds = 4" [10 cm] in stockinette stitch with larger needles, after wet blocking
18 sts and 26 rows = 4" [10 cm] in gansey patterns with larger needles, after wet blocking.

## Special abbreviations

sl 1: Sl 1 stitch purlwise with yarn in back.
C1R (cross 1 over 2, leans to the right): Slip 2 stitches onto cable needle (cn) and hold in back, k1, then k2 from cn.
C1L (cross 1 over 2, leans to the left): Slip 1 stitch onto cn and hold in front, k2, then k1 from cn.

## Cable panel (36 stitches)

for sizes -(42½, 48½, 54½, 60½, 66½, 72½)" [- (108, 123, 138.5, 153.5, 169, 184) cm] only

See also chart, page 81.
Set up row: (WS) K8, p6, (k2, p1) two times, k2, p6, k8.
Row 1: (RS) P2, k4, p2, C1R, C1L, (p2, sl 1) two times, p2, C1R, C1L, p2, k4, p2.
Row 2: K8, p6, (k2, p1) two times, k2, p6, k8.
Row 3: P2, k4, p2, k6, (p2, sl 1) two times, p2, k6, p2, k4, p2.
Row 4: Rep Row 2.
Row 5: Rep Row 1.
Row 6: K2, p4, k2, p6, (k2, p1) two times, k2, p6, k2, p4, k2.
Row 7: Rep Row 3.
Row 8: Rep Row 6.
Repeat Rows 1-8 for cable panel.

## Cable panel (33 stitches)

for size 36½ (-, -, -, -, -, -)" [92.5 (-, -, -, -, -, -) cm] only

See also chart, page 81.
Set up row: (WS) K8, p6, k2, p1, k2, p6, k8.
Row 1: (RS) P2, k4, p2, C1R, C1L, p2, sl 1, p2, C1R, C1L, p2, k4, p2.
Row 2: K8, p6, k2, p1, k2, p6, k8.
Row 3: P2, k4, p2, k6, p2, sl 1, p2, k6, p2, k4, p2.
Row 4: Rep Row 2.
Row 5: Rep Row 1.
Row 6: K2, p4, k2, p6, k2, p1, k2, p6, k2, p4, k2.
Row 7: Rep Row 3.
Row 8: Rep Row 6.
Repeat Rows 1-8 for cable panel.

## Eyelet panel (15 stitches)
See also chart, page 81.
**Row 1:** (RS) P2, k2, k2tog, yo, k3, yo, ssk, k2, p2.
**Row 2:** K2, p4, k3, p4, k2.
**Row 3:** P2, k1, k2tog, yo, k5, yo, ssk, k1, p2.
**Row 4:** K2, p3, k5, p3, k2.
**Row 5:** P2, k2tog, yo, k7, yo, ssk, p2.
**Row 6:** K2, p11, k2.
Repeat Rows 1-6 for eyelet panel.

## Sleeve panel (22 stitches)
See also chart, page 81.
**Set up rnd:** (P2, sl 1) two times, p2, k6, (p2, sl 1) two times, p2.
**Rnd 1:** (P2, k1) two times, p2, k6, (p2, k1) two times, p2.
**Rnd 2:** (P2, sl 1) two times, p2, k6, (p2, sl 1) two times, p2.
**Rnd 3:** (P2, k1) two times, p2, k6, (p2, k1) two times, p2.
**Rnd 4:** (P2, sl 1) two times, p2, C1L, C1R, (p2, sl 1) two times, p2.
Repeat Rnds 1-4 for sleeve panel.

## Note
Gansey is knitted in the round, from the bottom up to underarm, then front and back are worked flat with short row shaping and joined using the three-needle bind off. Stitches are picked up around armhole and worked in the round to cuff, with a small detail panel at top of sleeve. Stitches are picked up around neck edge and worked in a rib trim.

# gansey

With smaller, longer circular needle (circ) and using the long-tail cast on, CO 144 (168, 192, 216, 240, 264, 288) sts. Place marker (pm) for beg of rnd (BOR) and join to work in the rnd, careful not to twist sts.

## Begin broken rib
**First rnd:** Knit.
**Next rnd:** *K1, p1; rep from * to end.
Rep the last 2 rnds for 2¼" [5.5 cm], ending after a k1, p1 rnd.
**Next rnd** *inc rnd:* K1, m1, k71 (83, 95, 107, 119, 131, 143), pm for side, k1, m1, k71 (83, 95, 107, 119, 131, 143) sts to end (2 sts inc'd)—146 (170, 194, 218, 242, 266, 290) sts. BOR counts as second side marker. Change to larger circ.

## Begin stockinette
**Next rnd:** Knit.
Cont in St st until pc meas 14" [35.5 cm] from beg.

## Begin underarm shaping
**Next rnd** *inc rnd:* *K1, m1, knit to 1 st before side marker (m), m1, k1; rep from * one more time (4 sts inc'd)—150 (174, 198, 222, 246, 270, 294) sts.
Rep *inc rnd* every 4 rnds one more time, then every 2 rnds two times—162 (186, 210, 234, 258, 282, 306) sts on needle.

## Separate front and back
**Next rnd** *inc rnd:* Using the cable cast on, CO 7 sts, k16 (19, 25, 31, 34, 40, 46), m1, k9 (12, 12, 12, 12, 12, 12), m1, k45 (45, 45, 45, 51, 51, 51), m1, k9 (12, 12, 12, 12, 12, 12), m1, k9 (12, 18, 24, 27, 33, 39) sts to side m, then place rem sts for front onto waste yarn (4 sts inc'd).

## Back
**Next row** *place markers:* (WS) Using the cable cast on, CO 7 sts, k1, p1, (k2, p1) 1 (2, 4, 6, 7, 9, 11) times, pm for cable panel, work set up row of cable panel over next 33 (36, 36, 36, 36, 36, 36) sts, pm for cable panel, p1, (k2, p1) 1 (1, 1, 1, 2, 2, 2) times, pm for eyelet panel, p15, pm for eyelet panel, p1, (k2, p1) 1 (1, 1, 1, 2, 2, 2) times, pm for cable panel, work set up row of cable panel over next 33 (36, 36, 36, 36, 36, 36) sts, pm for cable panel, (p1, k2) 1 (2, 4, 6, 7, 9, 11) times, p1, k1—99 (111, 123, 135, 147, 159, 171) sts on needle.

## Begin gansey patterns
**Next row:** (RS) K1, sl 1, (p2, sl 1) to cable m, work Row 1 of cable panel to next m, sl 1, (p2, sl 1) to eyelet m, work Row 1 of eyelet panel to next m, sl 1, (p2, sl 1) to cable m, work Row 1 of cable panel to next m, sl 1, (p2, sl 1) to last st, k1.
**Next row:** K1, p1, (k2, p1) to cable m, work cable panel to next m, p1, (k2, p1) to eyelet m, work eyelet panel to next m, p1, (k2, p1) to cable m, work cable panel to next m, p1, (k2, p1) to last st, k1.
Cont as est until Rows 1-6 of eyelet panel have been worked 4 (4, 5, 6, 7, 8, 9) times, then work Rows 1-4 one time.

Piece meas approx 4¼ (4¼, 5¼, 6¼, 7, 8, 9)" [11 (11, 13.5, 16, 18, 20.5, 23) cm] from underarm.

## Begin shoulder shaping

Do not count yarnovers as stitches; as short rows approach cables, work cable stitches in stockinette stitch.

**Next row** *short row 1:* (RS) Work as est to last 5 (6, 7, 8, 8, 9, 10) sts, turn; (WS) yo, work as est to last 5 (6, 7, 8, 8, 9, 10) sts, turn.

**Next row** *short row 2:* (RS) Yo, work to 3 (4, 5, 6, 7, 8, 9) sts before last gap, turn; (WS) yo, work to 3 (4, 5, 6, 7, 8, 9) sts before last gap, turn.

Rep *short row two* 2 (2, 2, 2, 4, 4, 4) more times.

**Sizes - (-, -, -, 60½, 66½, 72½)" [- (-, -, -, 153.5, 169, 184) cm] only:**
Proceed to All sizes.

**Sizes 36½ (42½, 48½, 54½, -, -, -)" [92.5 (108, 123, 138.5, -, -, -) cm] only:**
**Next row** *short row 3:* (RS) Yo, work to 4 (5, 6, 7, -, -, -) sts before last gap, turn; (WS) yo, work to 4 (5, 6, 7, -, -, -) sts before last gap, turn.
Rep *short row 3* one more time.

## All sizes

**Next row:** (RS) Yo, work to end, working each yo tog with the st after gap: k2tog if a knit st and p2tog if a purl.

**Next row:** Work to end, working each yo tog with the st after gap: ssk if a knit st and ssp if a purl.

Break yarn, leaving a long tail at armhole edge for finishing. Place sts onto waste yarn.

## Front

Return sts held for front to larger circ.

**Next row** *inc row:* (RS) With RS of front facing and beg at left armhole edge, pick up and knit 7 sts in underarm CO from left back, k9 (12, 18, 24, 27, 33, 39), m1, k9 (12, 12, 12, 12, 12, 12), m1, k45 (45, 45, 45, 51, 51, 51), m1, k9 (12, 12, 12, 12, 12, 12), m1, k9 (12, 18, 24, 27, 33, 39) sts to end, then pick up and knit 7 sts in underarm CO from right back (4 sts inc'd)—99 (111, 123, 135, 147, 159, 171) sts on needle.

**Next row** *place markers:* K1, p1, (k2, p1) 1 (2, 4, 6, 7, 9, 11) times, pm for cable panel, work set up row of cable panel over next 33 (36, 36, 36, 36, 36, 36) sts, pm for cable panel, p1, (k2, p1) 1 (1, 1, 1, 2, 2, 2) times, pm for eyelet panel, p15, pm for eyelet panel, p1, (k2, p1) 1 (1, 1, 1, 2, 2, 2) times, pm for cable panel, work set up row of cable panel over next 33 (36, 36, 36, 36, 36, 36) sts, pm for cable panel, (p1, k2) 1 (2, 4, 6, 7, 9, 11) times, p1, k1.

## Begin gansey patterns

**Next row:** (RS) K1, sl 1, (p2, sl 1) to cable m, work Row 1 of cable panel to next m, sl 1, (p2, sl 1) to eyelet m, work Row 1 of eyelet panel to next m, sl 1, (p2, sl 1) to cable m, work Row 1 of cable panel to next m, sl 1, (p2, sl 1) to last st, k1.

**Next row:** K1, p1, (k2, p1) to cable m, work cable panel to next m, p1, (k2, p1) to eyelet m, work eyelet panel to next m, p1, (k2, p1) to cable m, work cable panel to next m, p1, (k2, p1) to last st, k1.

Cont as est until Rows 1-6 of eyelet panel have been worked a total of 4 (4, 5, 6, 7, 8, 9) times. Piece meas approx 3¾ (3¾, 4½, 5½, 6½, 7½, 8¼)" [9.5 (9.5, 11.5, 14, 16.5, 19, 21) cm] from underarm.

## Begin neck shaping

**Next row:** (RS) Work as est to eyelet m, join a new ball of yarn and BO all sts to next eyelet m, removing marker to BO last st, work as est to end—42 (48, 54, 60, 66, 72, 78) sts rem for each side.

**Next row:** Work to right neck edge; on left neck edge, work to end.

**Next row:** (RS) Work to neck edge; then BO 3 (3, 3, 3, 4, 4, 4) sts, work to end.

**Next row:** Work to neck edge; then BO 3 (3, 3, 3, 4, 4, 4) sts, work to end—39 (45, 51, 57, 62, 68, 74) sts rem each.

## Begin shoulder shaping

Do not count yarnovers as stitches; as short rows approach cables, work cable stitches in stockinette stitch.

**Next row** *short row 1:* (RS) Work to neck edge; then BO 2 (2, 2, 2, 3, 3, 3) sts, work to last 5 (6, 7, 8, 8, 9, 10) sts, turn; (WS) yo, work to neck edge; then BO 2 (2, 2, 2, 3, 3, 3) sts, work to last 5 (6, 7, 8, 8, 9, 10) sts, turn—37 (43, 49, 55, 59, 65, 71) sts rem each.

**Next row** *short row 2:* (RS) Yo, work to neck edge; then BO 2 (2, 2, 2, 3, 3, 3) sts, work to 3 (4, 5, 6, 7, 8, 9) sts before last gap, turn; (WS) yo, work to neck edge; then BO 2 (2, 2, 2, 3, 3, 3) sts, work to 3 (4, 5, 6, 7, 8, 9) sts before last gap, turn—35 (41, 47, 53, 56, 62, 68) sts rem each.

**Next row** *short row 3:* (RS) Yo, work to 2 sts before neck edge, ssk; then k2tog, work to 3 (4, 5, 6, 7, 8, 9) sts before last gap, turn; (WS) yo, work to neck edge; then work to 3 (4, 5, 6, 7, 8, 9) sts before last gap, turn—34 (40, 46, 52, 55, 61, 67) sts rem each.

Rep *short row 3* one more time—33 (39, 45, 51, 54, 60, 66) sts rem each.

**Next row** *short row 4:* (RS) Yo, work to neck edge; then work to 4 (5, 6, 7, 7, 8, 9) sts before last gap, turn; (WS) yo, work to neck edge; then work to 4 (5, 6, 7, 7, 8, 9) sts before last gap, turn.

### Sizes 36½ (42½, 48½, 54½, -, -, -)" [92.5 (108, 123, 138.5, -, -, -) cm] only:

**Next row** *short row 5:* (RS) Yo, work to 2 sts before neck edge, ssk; then k2tog, work to 4 (5, 6, 7, -, -, -) sts before last gap, turn; (WS) yo, work to neck edge; then work to 4 (5, 6, 7, -, -, -) sts before last gap, turn—32 (38, 44, 50, -, -, -) sts rem each.

Proceed to All sizes.

### Sizes - (-, -, -, 60½, 66½, 72½)" [- (-, -, -, 153.5, 169, 184) cm] only:

**Next row:** Rep *short row 3*— - (-, -, -, 53, 59, 65) sts rem each.

### All sizes

32 (38, 44, 50, 53, 59, 65) sts rem for each side.

**Next row:** (RS) Yo, work to neck edge; then work to end, working each yo tog with the st after gap: k2tog if a knit st and p2tog if a purl.

**Next row:** Work to neck edge; then work to end, working each yo tog with the st after gap: ssk if a knit st and ssp if a purl.

Break yarn at neck edge only.

## Join shoulders

Place sts held for back onto smaller circ. With RS of pcs tog and attached yarn, using the three-needle bind off, BO all left front shoulder sts with corresponding back sts. With long tail at right armhole edge, rep for right shoulder, then BO rem back neck sts.

Gently steam block piece.

## Sleeves

With RS facing and larger double-pointed needles (dpns), beg at underarm, pick up and knit 22 (22, 26, 30, 34, 38, 42) sts to shoulder seam (approx 3 sts for every 4 rows), then pick up and knit 22 (22, 26, 30, 34, 38, 42) sts to underarm—44 (44, 52, 60, 68, 76, 84) sts on needles. Pm for BOR.

**First rnd** *place markers:* K11 (11, 15, 19, 23, 27, 31), pm for panel, work set up rnd of sleeve panel over next 22 sts, pm for panel, k11 (11, 15, 19, 23, 27, 31) sts to end.

## Begin sleeve panel

**Next rnd:** Knit to panel m, work Rnd 1 of sleeve panel to next m, knit to end.

Cont as est until Rnds 1-4 of panel have been worked two times.

## Begin sleeve shaping

**Next rnd** *dec rnd:* K1, k2tog, knit to panel m, work Rnd 1 of sleeve panel to next m, knit to last 3 sts, ssk, k1 (2 sts dec'd)—42 (42, 50, 58, 66, 74, 82) sts rem. Remove panel markers on next rnd and cont in St st.

Rep *dec rnd* every 8 (8, 6, 4, 2, 2, 2) rnds 1 (1, 3, 4, 1, 5, 9) more times, then every 10 (10, 8, 6, 4, 4, 4) rnds 5 (5, 5, 7, 14, 12, 10) times—30 (30, 34, 36, 36, 40, 44) sts rem.

Cont in St st until sleeve meas 14" [35.5 cm] from pick-up.

Change to smaller dpns.

## Begin cuff trim

**Next rnd:** *K1, p1; rep from * to end.
**Next rnd:** Knit.
Rep the last 2 rnds for 1¾" [4.5 cm], ending after a knit rnd.
**Next rnd:** Bind off in pattern.

## Finishing

Weave in ends. Wet block gansey to finished measurements.

## Neck trim

With RS facing and smaller, shorter circ, beg at center of back neck, pick up and knit 1 st in each BO st and 1 st in each row around neck edge, making sure to pick up an even number of sts. Pm for BOR.
**First rnd:** *K1, p1; rep from * to end.
Cont in rib for 1" [2.5 cm].
**Next rnd:** Bind off in pattern.

Weave in rem ends and block again, if you like.

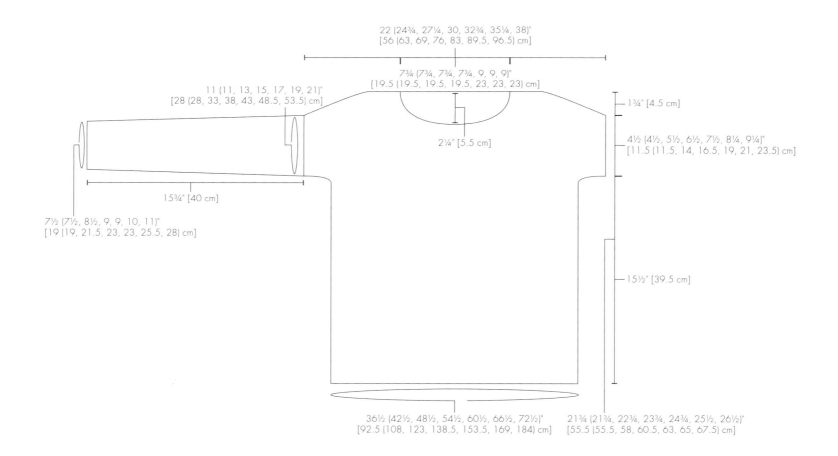

22 (24¾, 27¼, 30, 32¾, 35¼, 38)"
[56 (63, 69, 76, 83, 89.5, 96.5) cm]

7¾ (7¾, 7¾, 7¾, 9, 9, 9)"
[19.5 (19.5, 19.5, 19.5, 23, 23, 23) cm]

11 (11, 13, 15, 17, 19, 21)"
[28 (28, 33, 38, 43, 48.5, 53.5) cm]

1¾" [4.5 cm]

2¼" [5.5 cm]

4½ (4½, 5½, 6½, 7½, 8¼, 9¼)"
[11.5 (11.5, 14, 16.5, 19, 21, 23.5) cm]

15¾" [40 cm]

7½ (7½, 8½, 9, 9, 10, 11)"
[19 (19, 21.5, 23, 23, 25.5, 28) cm]

15½" [39.5 cm]

36½ (42½, 48½, 54½, 60½, 66½, 72½)"
[92.5 (108, 123, 138.5, 153.5, 169, 184) cm]

21¾ (21¾, 22¾, 23¾, 24¾, 25½, 26½)"
[55.5 (55.5, 58, 60.5, 63, 65, 67.5) cm]

## Eyelet panel

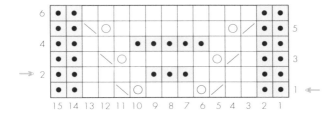

## Sleeve panel

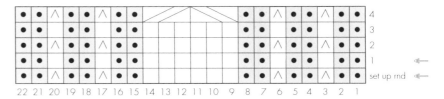

## Cable panel for size 36½ (-, -, -, -, -, -)" [92.5 (-, -, -, -, -, -) cm] only

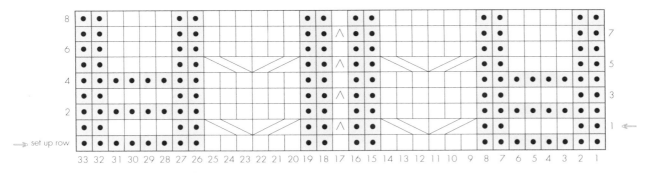

## Cable panel for sizes - (42½, 48½, 54½, 60½, 66½, 72½)" [- (108, 123, 138.5, 153.5, 169, 184) cm] only

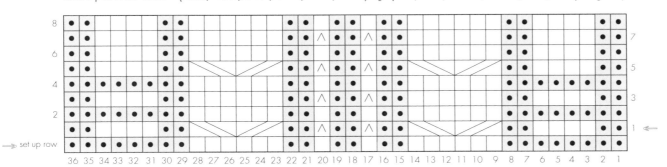

## Key

| | |
|---|---|
| ☐ | knit on RS, purl on WS |
| ● | purl on RS, knit on WS |
| ⋀ | sl 1 |
| ○ | yo |
| ╱ | k2tog |
| ╲ | ssk |
| ⫽ | C1R |
| ⧅ | C1L |

# aspen

Slipped stitches are one of my favorite ways to add color to a knitted piece without having to work with two yarn strands at the same time. In slipped-stitch patterns, you work only one color at a time on a row, slipping a stitch or two depending on the pattern. On the next row, when you change to a new color, the slipped stitches bring the first color into the row with the second. Slipped stitches can create texture as well as color patterns: in this instance, drawing up and knitting a stitch six rows below makes waves across the yoke.

## Finished measurements
31 (35, 39, 43, 47, 51, 55, 59)" [78.5 (89, 99, 109, 119.5, 129.5, 139.5, 150) cm] bust circumference; shown in size 35" [89 cm] on a 32" [81.5 cm], 5'10" [178 cm] tall model (3" [7.5 cm] positive ease)

## Yarn
Owl by Quince & Co
(50% American wool, 50% alpaca; 120yd [110 m]/50g)
- 5 (5, 6, 7, 7, 8, 9, 9) skeins Snowy 300 (MC)
- 1 skein Albertine 306 (CC)

## Needles
- One 32" circular needle (circ) in size US 9 [5.5 mm]
- One 32" circ in size US 8 [5 mm]
- One 16" circ in size US 8 [5 mm]
- One set double-pointed needles in size US 9 [5.5 mm]

Or size to obtain gauge

## Notions
- Stitch markers
- Waste yarn
- Tapestry needle

## Gauge
16 sts and 24 rnds = 4" [10 cm] in stockinette stitch with larger needles, after wet blocking
17 sts and 39 rnds = 4" [10 cm] in yoke pattern with smaller needles, after wet blocking.

## Special abbreviation
**lifted stitch:** Insert RH needle tip, from the bottom up, into the purl stitch 6 rows below next stitch on needle, lift stitch onto LH needle. Knit the lifted stitch, knit the next stitch, then pass lifted stitch over it. See page 108 for an illustrated tutorial.

## Yoke pattern (multiple of 8 sts, decreases to 6)
See also chart, page 85.
**Rnd 1:** With CC, knit.
**Rnd 2:** With MC, purl.
**Rnd 3:** With MC, knit.
**Rnds 4-7:** With CC, knit.
**Rnd 8:** With MC, purl.
**Rnd 9:** With MC, *k7, then work lifted st with next st; rep from * to end.
**Rnds 10-14:** Rep Rnds 4-8.
**Rnd 15:** With MC, *k3, then work lifted st with next st, k4; rep from * to end.
**Rnds 16-19:** Rep Rnds 4-7.
**Rnd 20** *dec rnd:* With MC, *p1, p2tog-tbl, p2, p2tog, p1; rep from * to end (2 sts dec'd for each pattern repeat).
**Rnd 21:** With MC, *k5, then work lifted st with next st; rep from * to end.
**Rnds 22-25:** With CC, knit.
**Rnd 26:** With MC, purl.
**Rnd 27:** With MC, *k2, then work lifted st with next st, k3; rep from * to end.
**Rnds 28-32:** Rep Rnds 22-26.
**Rnd 33:** Rep Rnd 21.

## Notes
1. Body is knitted in the round from the bottom up to underarm. Stitches are held for underarm, then cast on to waste yarn to later become the sleeves. Yoke is continued to neck edge first with raglan shaping, then in a two-color lifted stitch pattern with round yoke shaping. Stitches are picked up from waste yarn and worked in the round to cuff.
2. When picking up live stitches from the bottom edge of a cast on, you will have one more stitch than the number you cast on. See page 109 for an illustrated tutorial.

# pullover

With MC and larger circular needle (circ), using the long-tail cast on, CO 124 (140, 156, 172, 188, 204, 220, 236) sts. Place marker (pm) for beg of rnd (BOR) and join to work in the rnd, careful not to twist sts.

## Begin at bottom edge

**First rnd** *place markers:* K62 (70, 78, 86, 94, 102, 110, 118), pm for side, k62 (70, 78, 86, 94, 102, 110, 118) sts to end (BOR counts as second side marker).
Cont in St st for 2½ (2½, 2½, 3, 3, 3, 3½, 3½)" [6.5 (6.5, 6.5, 7.5, 7.5, 7.5, 9, 9) cm].

## Begin side shaping

**Next rnd** *dec rnd:* *K2, k2tog, knit to 4 sts before side marker (m), ssk, k2; rep from * one more time (4 sts dec'd)—120 (136, 152, 168, 184, 200, 216, 232) sts rem.
Knit 16 rnds.
**Next rnd:** Rep *dec rnd*—116 (132, 148, 164, 180, 196, 212, 228) sts rem.
Knit 14 rnds.
**Next rnd** *inc rnd:* *K2, m1, knit to 2 sts before m, m1, k2; rep from * one more time (4 sts inc'd)—120 (136, 152, 168, 184, 200, 216, 232) sts.
Knit 14 rnds.
**Next rnd:** Rep *inc rnd*—124 (140, 156, 172, 188, 204, 220, 236) sts.
Cont in St st until pc meas 12 (12, 12, 12½, 12½, 12½, 13, 13)" [30.5 (30.5, 30.5, 32, 32, 32, 33, 33) cm] from beg.

**Next rnd:** *Knit to side m, remove m, k4 (5, 6, 6, 6, 7, 7, 8), then place last 8 (10, 12, 12, 12, 14, 14, 16) sts onto waste yarn; rep from * one more time—54 (60, 66, 74, 82, 88, 96, 102) sts rem each for front and back.

## Begin yoke

**Next rnd:** K27 (30, 33, 37, 41, 44, 48, 51), pm for new BOR, k27 (30, 33, 37, 41, 44, 48, 51), turn work, with waste yarn, make slipknot (first sleeve st), place onto RH needle, and using the backward loop cast on, CO 37 (39, 41, 43, 47, 49, 53, 55) more sts for sleeve, turn work, pm for raglan, with MC, knit sts cast on for sleeve, pm for raglan, knit across front sts, turn work, with waste yarn, make slipknot (first sleeve st), place onto RH needle, and using the backward loop cast on, CO 37 (39, 41, 43, 47, 49, 53, 55) more sts for sleeve, turn work, pm for raglan, with MC, knit sts cast on for sleeve, pm for raglan, k27 (30, 33, 37, 41, 44, 48, 51) sts to end—184 (200, 216, 236, 260, 276, 300, 316) sts on needle.
**First rnd:** Knit.
Knit 2 more rnds.

## Begin raglan shaping

**Next rnd** *dec rnd:* *Knit to 3 sts before m, ssk, k1, slip marker (sl m), k1, k2tog; rep from * three more times, knit to end (8 sts dec'd)—176 (192, 208, 228, 252, 268, 292, 308) sts rem.
Rep *dec rnd* every 2 rnds 0 (0, 2, 0, 4, 4, 4, 4) more times, every 3 rnds 0 (4, 4, 6, 5, 7, 8, 10) times, then every 4 rnds 2 (0, 0, 0, 0, 0, 0, 0) times—160 (160, 160, 180, 180, 180, 196, 196) sts rem; 48 (50, 52, 60, 62, 64, 70, 72) sts each for front and back and 32 (30, 28, 30, 28, 26, 28, 26) sts for each sleeve.
Knit 3 rnds, removing raglan markers on final rnd.

## Begin round yoke shaping

**Next rnd** *dec rnd:* With CC, *k8 (8, 8, 7, 7, 7, 47, 47), k2tog; rep from * to end; 16 (16, 16, 20, 20, 20, 4, 4) sts dec'd—144 (144, 144, 160, 160, 160, 192, 192) sts rem.
Change to smaller, longer circ.

## Begin yoke pattern

Change to smaller, shorter circ when necessary.
**Next rnd:** Work Rnd 1 of yoke pattern to end.
Cont as est until Rnds 1-33 have been worked—108 (108, 108, 120, 120, 120, 144, 144) sts rem.
Break CC.

## Continue round yoke shaping

**Next rnd** *dec rnd:* *K10, k2tog; rep from * to end; 9 (9, 9, 10, 10, 10, 12, 12) sts dec'd—99 (99, 99, 110, 110, 110, 132, 132) sts rem.
Knit 1 rnd.
**Next rnd** *dec rnd:* *K9, k2tog; rep from * to end—90 (90, 90, 100, 100, 100, 120, 120) sts rem.
Knit 1 rnd.
**Next rnd** *dec rnd:* *K8, k2tog; rep from * to end—81 (81, 81, 90, 90, 90, 108, 108) sts rem.

**Sizes 31 (35, 39, 43, 47, 51, -, -)" [78.5 (89, 99, 109, 119.5, 129.5, -, -) cm] only:**
**Next rnd:** Bind off purlwise.

**Sizes - (-, -, -, -, -, 55, 59)" [- (-, -, -, -, -, 139.5, 150) cm] only:**
Knit 1 rnd.
**Next rnd** *dec rnd:* *K7, k2tog; rep from * to end—96 sts rem.
**Next rnd:** Bind off purlwise.

## Sleeves

With MC, RS facing, and double-pointed needles, place first 4 (5, 6, 6, 6, 7, 7, 8) sts held for underarm onto needle, pm for BOR, place rem 4 (5, 6, 6, 6, 7, 7, 8) underarm sts onto needle, then, working one st at a time, pick out waste yarn from sleeve cast on and place each st onto needle—47 (51, 55, 57, 61, 65, 69, 73) sts on needles.

**First rnd:** Knit.

Cont in St st until sleeve meas 1¼" [3 cm] from underarm.

## Begin sleeve shaping

**Next rnd** *dec rnd:* K2, k2tog, knit to last 4 sts, ssk, k2 (2 sts dec'd)—45 (49, 53, 55, 59, 63, 67, 71) sts rem.

Rep *dec rnd* every 10 (8, 6, 6, 4, 4, 4, 4) rnds 2 (6, 2, 5, 1, 3, 6, 7) more times, then every 12 (10, 8, 8, 6, 6, 6, 6) rnds 4 (2, 7, 5, 11, 10, 8, 8) times—33 (33, 35, 35, 35, 37, 39, 41) sts rem.

Cont in St st until sleeve meas 17" [43 cm] from underarm.

**Next rnd:** Bind off purlwise.

## Finishing

Weave in ends. Wet block pullover to finished measurements.

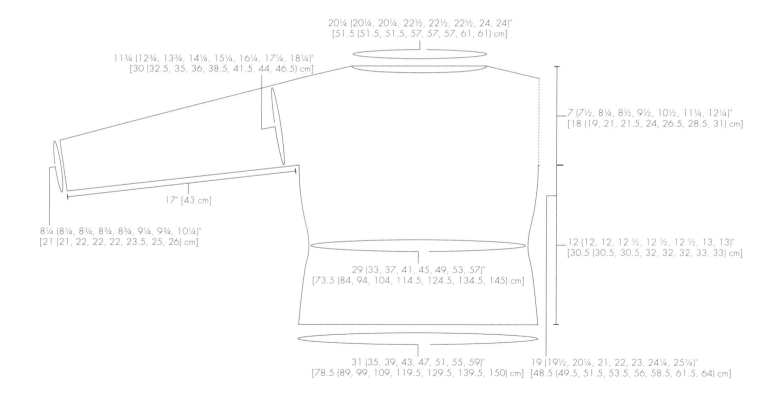

20¼ (20¼, 20¼, 22½, 22½, 22½, 24, 24)"
[51.5 (51.5, 51.5, 57, 57, 57, 61, 61) cm]

11¾ (12¾, 13¾, 14¼, 15¼, 16¼, 17¼, 18¼)"
[30 (32.5, 35, 36, 38.5, 41.5, 44, 46.5) cm]

7 (7½, 8¼, 8½, 9½, 10½, 11¼, 12¼)"
[18 (19, 21, 21.5, 24, 26.5, 28.5, 31) cm]

17" [43 cm]

8¼ (8¼, 8¾, 8¾, 8¾, 9¼, 9¾, 10¼)"
[21 (21, 22, 22, 22, 23.5, 25, 26) cm]

12 (12, 12, 12½, 12½, 12½, 13, 13)"
[30.5 (30.5, 30.5, 32, 32, 32, 33, 33) cm]

29 (33, 37, 41, 45, 49, 53, 57)"
[73.5 (84, 94, 104, 114.5, 124.5, 134.5, 145) cm]

31 (35, 39, 43, 47, 51, 55, 59)"
[78.5 (89, 99, 109, 119.5, 129.5, 139.5, 150) cm]

19 (19½, 20¼, 21, 22, 23, 24¼, 25¼)"
[48.5 (49.5, 51.5, 53.5, 56, 58.5, 61.5, 64) cm]

## Yoke pattern

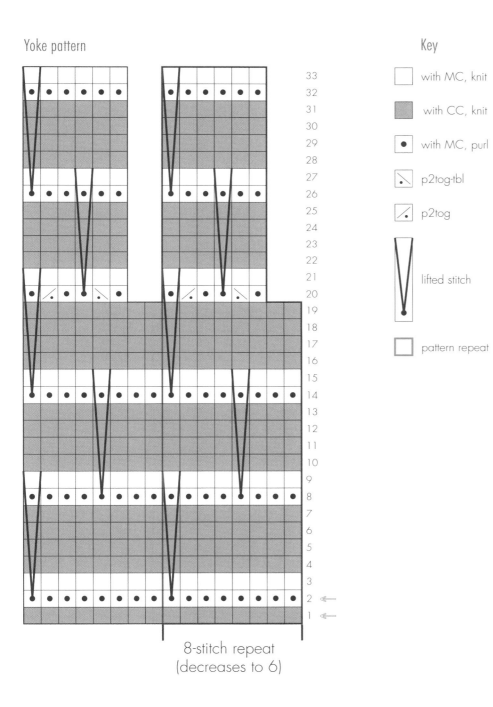

33
32
31
30
29
28
27
26
25
24
23
22
21
20
19
18
17
16
15
14
13
12
11
10
9
8
7
6
5
4
3
2
1

8-stitch repeat
(decreases to 6)

## Key

☐  with MC, knit

▨  with CC, knit

•  with MC, purl

◢  p2tog-tbl

◣  p2tog

⋁  lifted stitch

☐  pattern repeat

# larch

Larch's body is a simple rectangle, almost as wide as it is tall. The sweater has the handiest of pockets, the cushiest of deep cowl necks. Just a few inches of simple rib anchor the bottom edge and cuffs. Other than that, you could read *War and Peace* while you cruise in stockinette stitch.

In an ample width, it makes one want to spread arms, swing around, and practice a pirouette. In a version that fits closer to the body, it would still be a comfortable, wear-it-all-the-time pullover. Note that we've sized it from 33" to 70"—so you can make it narrow and clingy or wide and swingy, depending on your preference.

## Finished measurements
33 (37¼, 41¼, 45½, 49½, 53¾, 57¾, 62, 66, 70¼)" [84 (94.5, 105, 115.5, 125.5, 136.5, 146.5, 157.5, 167.5, 178.5) cm] bust circumference; shown in size 49½" [125.5 cm] on a 32" [81.5 cm], 5'10" [178 cm] tall model (17½" [44.5 cm] positive ease)

## Yarn
### Owl by Quince & Co
(50% American wool, 50% alpaca; 120yd [110m]/50g)
- 9 (10, 10, 11, 12, 13, 14, 15, 15, 16) skeins Albertine 306

## Needles
- One 32" circular needle (circ) in size US 7 [4.5 mm]
- One 24" circ in size US 7 [4.5 mm]
- One set double-pointed needles in size US 7 [4.5 mm]

Or size to obtain gauge

## Notions
- Stitch markers
- Waste yarn
- Tapestry needle

## Gauge
15½ sts and 23 rnds = 4" [10 cm] in stockinette stitch, after wet blocking.

## Special abbreviation
sl 1: Slip 1 stitch purlwise with yarn in back.

## Note
Pullover is worked in the round, from the bottom up to underarm with inset pockets. Front and back are worked flat to shoulders with short row shaping, then joined using the three-needle bind off. Stitches are picked up around armhole edge and knitted in the round to cuff. Stitches are picked up around neck edge and worked for cowl.

# pullover

## Pocket lining (Make 2)
With shorter circular needle (circ), or if you prefer, work back and forth on two double-pointed needles (dpns), using the long-tail cast on, CO 22 sts.
First row: (RS) Knit.
Cont in St st for 4¼" [11 cm], ending after a WS row.
Next row: (RS) BO 1 st, knit to end.
Next row: BO 1 st, purl to end—20 sts rem.
Break yarn. Place sts onto waste yarn.

## Body
With longer circ and using the long-tail cast on, CO 128 (144, 160, 176, 192, 208, 224, 240, 256, 272) sts. Place marker (pm) for beg of rnd (BOR) and join to work in the rnd, careful not to twist sts.

## Begin rib trim
First rnd: *K1, p1; rep from * to end.
Cont in rib for 2" [5 cm].

## Begin stockinette
Next rnd: Knit.
Cont in St st until pc meas 9¼" [23.5 cm] from beg.
Next rnd *place markers:* K3 (5, 9, 11, 15, 19, 21, 25, 27, 31), pm for pocket, k20, pm for pocket, k18 (22, 22, 26, 26, 26, 30, 30, 34, 34), pm for pocket, k20, pm for pocket, k3 (5, 9, 11, 15, 19, 21, 25, 27, 31), pm for side, k64 (72, 80, 88, 96, 104, 112, 120, 128, 136) sts to end (BOR counts as second side marker).

## Begin pocket openings

**Next rnd:** *Knit to pocket marker (m), BO all sts to next m, removing marker to BO last st; rep from * one more time, knit to end, keeping side m in place.

**Next rnd:** With RS of all pcs facing, *knit to pocket opening, place sts for pocket onto LH needle and knit across; rep from * one more time, knit to end.

## Continue stockinette

**Next rnd:** Knit.

Cont in St st until pc meas 17" [43 cm] from beg.

## Begin underarm shaping

**Next rnd** *inc rnd:* *K1, M1L, knit to 1 st before side m, M1R, k1; rep from * one more time (4 sts inc'd)—132 (148, 164, 180, 196, 212, 228, 244, 260, 276) sts.

Rep *inc rnd* every 4 rnds one more time, then every 2 rnds one time—140 (156, 172, 188, 204, 220, 236, 252, 268, 284) sts on needle. Knit 1 rnd.

## Separate front and back

Using the cable cast on, CO 7 (7, 7, 7, 7, 4, 4, 4, 4, 4) sts, knit to side m, then place rem sts for back onto waste yarn.

## Front

**Next row:** (WS) Using the cable cast on, CO 7 (7, 7, 7, 7, 4, 4, 4, 4, 4) sts, purl to end—84 (92, 100, 108, 116, 118, 126, 134, 142, 150) sts on needle.

**Next row:** Knit.

Cont in St st until pc meas 6 (6½, 7, 7¼, 7½, 7¾, 8, 8½, 8¾, 9)" [15 (16.5, 18, 18.5, 19, 19.5, 20.5, 21.5, 22, 23) cm] from underarm, ending after a RS row.

**Next row** *place markers:* (WS) P37 (41, 44, 48, 51, 52, 56, 60, 64, 68), pm for neck, p10 (10, 12, 12, 14, 14, 14, 14, 14, 14), pm for neck, p37 (41, 44, 48, 51, 52, 56, 60, 64, 68) sts to end.

## Begin neck shaping

**Next row:** (RS) Knit to m, join a new ball of yarn and BO all sts to next m, removing marker to BO last st, knit to end—37 (41, 44, 48, 51, 52, 56, 60, 64, 68) sts rem for each side.

**Next row:** Purl to right neck edge; on left neck edge, sl 1, purl to end.

## Begin shoulder shaping

Do not count yarnovers as stitches.

**Next row** *short row 1:* (RS) Knit to neck edge; then BO 3 sts, knit to last 4 (4, 4, 5, 5, 5, 6, 6, 6, 6) sts, turn; (WS) yo, purl to neck edge; then BO 3 sts, purl to last 4 (4, 4, 5, 5, 5, 6, 6, 6, 6) sts, turn—34 (38, 41, 45, 48, 49, 53, 57, 61, 65) sts rem each.

**Next row** *short row 2:* (RS) Yo, knit to neck edge; then BO 2 sts, knit to 2 (3, 3, 3, 4, 4, 4, 5, 5, 6) sts before last gap, turn; (WS) yo, purl to neck edge; then BO 2 sts, purl to 2 (3, 3, 3, 4, 4, 4, 5, 5, 6) sts before last gap, turn—32 (36, 39, 43, 46, 47, 51, 55, 59, 63) sts rem each.

Rep *short row 2* one more time—30 (34, 37, 41, 44, 45, 49, 53, 57, 61) sts rem each.

**Next row** *short row 3:* (RS) Yo, knit to 2 sts before neck edge, ssk; then k2tog, knit to 3 (3, 4, 4, 4, 4, 5, 5, 6, 6) sts before last gap, turn; (WS) yo, purl to neck edge; then purl to 3 (3, 4, 4, 4, 4, 5, 5, 6, 6) sts before last gap, turn (2 sts dec'd)—29 (33, 36, 40, 43, 44, 48, 52, 56, 60) sts rem each.

Rep *short row 3* three more times—26 (30, 33, 37, 40, 41, 45, 49, 53, 57) sts rem each.

**Next row** *short row 4:* (RS) Yo, knit to neck edge; then knit to 3 (4, 4, 4, 5, 5, 5, 6, 6, 7) sts before last gap, turn; (WS) yo, purl to neck edge; then purl to 3 (4, 4, 4, 5, 5, 5, 6, 6, 7) sts before last gap, turn.

**Next row:** (RS) Yo, knit to neck edge; then knit to end, k2tog each yo with the st after gap.

**Next row:** Purl to neck edge; then purl to end, ssp each yo with the st after gap.

Break yarn. Place sts onto waste yarn.

## Back

Return sts held for back to longer circ.

**Next row:** (RS) With RS of back facing and beg at right armhole edge, pick up and knit 7 (7, 7, 7, 7, 4, 4, 4, 4, 4) sts in underarm CO from right front, knit across back sts, then pick up and knit 7 (7, 7, 7, 7, 4, 4, 4, 4, 4) sts in underarm CO from left front—84 (92, 100, 108, 116, 118, 126, 134, 142, 150) sts on needle.

**Next row:** Purl.

Cont in St st until pc meas 6¼ (6¾, 7¼, 7½, 7¾, 8, 8¼, 8¾, 9, 9¼)" [16 (17, 18.5, 19, 19.5, 20.5, 21, 22, 23, 23.5) cm] from underarm, ending after a RS row.

**Next row** *place markers:* (WS) P26 (30, 33, 37, 40, 41, 45, 49, 53, 57), pm for neck, p32 (32, 34, 34, 36, 36, 36, 36, 36, 36), pm for neck, p26 (30, 33, 37, 40, 41, 45, 49, 53, 57) sts to end.

## Begin shoulder shaping

**Next row** *short row 1:* (RS) Knit to last 4 (4, 4, 5, 5, 5, 6, 6, 6, 6) sts, turn; (WS) yo, purl to last 4 (4, 4, 5, 5, 5, 6, 6, 6, 6) sts, turn.

**Next row** *short row 2:* (RS) Yo, knit to 2 (3, 3, 3, 4, 4, 4, 5, 5, 6) sts before last gap, turn; (WS) yo, purl to 2 (3, 3, 3, 4, 4, 4, 5, 5, 6) sts before last gap, turn.

Rep *short row two* 1 (5, 1, 1, 5, 5, 1, 5, 1, 5) more times.

**Next row** *short row 3:* (RS) Yo, knit to 3 (4, 4, 4, 5, 5, 5, 6, 6, 7) sts before last gap, turn; (WS) yo, purl to 3 (4, 4, 4, 5, 5, 5, 6, 6, 7) sts before last gap, turn.

Rep *short row three* 4 (0, 4, 4, 0, 0, 4, 0, 4, 0) more times.

**Next row:** (RS) Yo, knit to end, k2tog each yo with the st after gap.

**Next row:** Purl to end, ssp each yo with the st after gap.

Break yarn at neck edge only.

## Join shoulders

Place sts held for front shoulders to shorter circ. With RS of pcs tog and attached yarn, using the three-needle bind off, BO all right front sts with corresponding back sts to neck m, BO sts for back to next m, then using the three-needle bind off, BO all left front sts with rem back sts.

Gently steam block piece.

## Sleeves

With RS facing and dpns, beg at center of underarm, pick up and knit 26 (28, 30, 31, 32, 33, 34, 36, 37, 38) sts to shoulder seam (approx 2 sts for every 3 rows), then pick up and knit 26 (28, 30, 31, 32, 33, 34, 36, 37, 38) sts to underarm. Pm for BOR.

**First rnd:** Knit.

Cont in St st until sleeve meas 1½" [4 cm] from pick-up.

## Begin sleeve shaping

**Next rnd** *dec rnd:* K1, k2tog, knit to last 3 sts, ssk, k1 (2 sts dec'd)—50 (54, 58, 60, 62, 64, 66, 70, 74, 76) sts rem.

Rep *dec rnd* every 4 rnds 1 (3, 6, 6, 7, 7, 9, 9, 11, 11) more times, then every 6 rnds 8 (7, 5, 5, 4, 4, 3, 3, 2, 2) times—32 (34, 36, 38, 40, 42, 42, 46, 48, 50) sts rem.

Cont in St st until sleeve meas 13¼" [33.5 cm] from pick-up.

## Begin cuff trim

**Next rnd:** *K1, p1; rep from * to end.
Cont in rib for 2" [5 cm].
**Next rnd:** Bind off in pattern.

## Finishing

Weave in ends. Wet block pullover to finished measurements.

## Cowl

With RS facing and shorter circ, beg at center of back neck, pick up 1 st in each BO st and 1 st for every 2 rows around neck edge.
**First rnd:** Knit.
Cont in St st until cowl meas 9¼" [23.5 cm] from pick-up.
**Next rnd:** Bind off loosely knitwise.

Weave in rem ends and block again, if you like.

Blocking is the magical move that takes an otherwise lumpy, curling piece of knitting and turns it into knitters' gold, a fabric smooth and even. Just as important, blocking coaxes out a yarn's best qualities, it plumps and adds loft to individual stitches and encourages a soft halo.

For Owl, in general, and in particular Larch, with its relaxed gauge for drape and swing, wet blocking is best. Fill a tub with tepid water and add a little wool soap and your sweater. Swish around and gently squeeze out extra water. Then lay out on a large towel and roll it up softly, but leave a little moisture, otherwise you'll block in wrinkles. Lay the sweater out on a flat surface to dry. If you want to speed things up, angle a window fan at your now smooth, soft sweater and it'll be dry in no time.

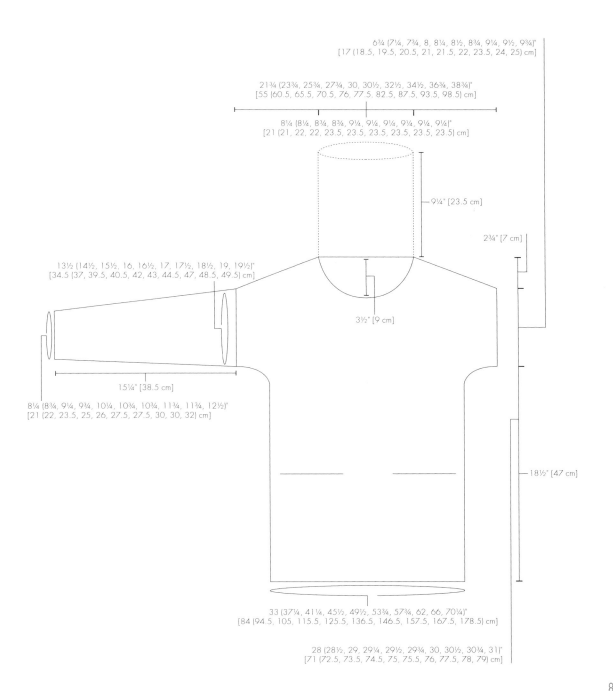

6¾ (7¼, 7¾, 8, 8¼, 8½, 8¾, 9¼, 9½, 9¾)"
[17 (18.5, 19.5, 20.5, 21, 21.5, 22, 23.5, 24, 25) cm]

21¾ (23¾, 25¾, 27¾, 30, 30½, 32½, 34½, 36¾, 38¾)"
[55 (60.5, 65.5, 70.5, 76, 77.5, 82.5, 87.5, 93.5, 98.5) cm]

8¼ (8¼, 8¾, 8¾, 9¼, 9¼, 9¼, 9¼, 9¼, 9¼)"
[21 (21, 22, 22, 23.5, 23.5, 23.5, 23.5, 23.5, 23.5) cm]

9¼" [23.5 cm]

2¾" [7 cm]

13½ (14½, 15½, 16, 16½, 17, 17½, 18½, 19, 19½)"
[34.5 (37, 39.5, 40.5, 42, 43, 44.5, 47, 48.5, 49.5) cm]

3½" [9 cm]

15¼" [38.5 cm]

8¼ (8¾, 9¼, 9¾, 10¼, 10¾, 10¾, 11¾, 11¾, 12½)"
[21 (22, 23.5, 25, 26, 27.5, 27.5, 30, 30, 32) cm]

18½" [47 cm]

33 (37¼, 41¼, 45½, 49½, 53¾, 57¾, 62, 66, 70¼)"
[84 (94.5, 105, 115.5, 125.5, 136.5, 146.5, 157.5, 167.5, 178.5) cm]

28 (28½, 29, 29¼, 29½, 29¾, 30, 30½, 30¾, 31)"
[71 (72.5, 73.5, 74.5, 75, 75.5, 76, 77.5, 78, 79) cm]

# walnut

An all-round workhorse is the Walnut Cardigan. It has deep pockets, a high cozy neck, and a vented side seam for ease of motion. I especially like the slim sleeves and smooth shoulder. And four buttons are plenty for a piece like this—they keep the cardigan closed on the top half and allow for graceful ease of movement below. The deep border and cuffs are worked in half brioche— a favorite variation on the classic brioche rib. Half brioche has a bit more stability than its stretchy cousin full brioche, and I love the plump stitches it makes on one of its sides.

## Finished measurements
35¼ (38, 41, 43¾, 46½, 49½, 52¼, 55)" [89.5 (96.5, 104, 111, 118, 125.5, 132.5, 139.5) cm] bust circumference; shown in size 38" [96.5 cm] on a 32" [81.5 cm], 5'10" [178 cm] tall model (6" [15 cm] positive ease)

## Yarn
Owl by Quince & Co
(50% American wool, 50% alpaca; 120yd [110m]/50g)
- 10 (11, 12, 12, 13, 14, 15, 16) skeins Sokoke 304

## Needles
- One 32" circular needle (circ) in size US 9 [5.5 mm]
- One 32" circ in size US 8 [5 mm]
- One 24" circ in size US 7 [4.5 mm]
- One set double-pointed needles (dpns) in size US 9 [5.5 mm]
- One set dpns in size US 8 [5 mm]

Or size to obtain gauge

## Notions
- Stitch markers
- Locking stitch markers
- Waste yarn
- Tapestry needle
- 3-6 buttons, ¾" [19 mm] [see note 2]

## Gauge
17 sts and 24 rows = 4" [10 cm] in reverse stockinette stitch with largest needles, after wet blocking
15 sts and 36 rows = 4" [10 cm] in half brioche stitch with middle-sized needles, after wet blocking.

## Special abbreviation
sl 1: Slip 1 stitch knitwise with yarn in back.

## Half brioche stitch
*Worked flat (odd number of stitches)*
Row 1: (RS) Sl 1, *k1, sl1yo; rep from * to last 2 sts, k2.
Row 2: Sl 1, *p1, brk; rep from * to last 2 sts, p1, k1.
Repeat Rows 1 and 2 for half brioche stitch.

*In the round (even number of stitches)*
Rnd 1: *K1, sl1yo; rep from * to end.
Rnd 2: *K1, brp; rep from * to end.
Repeat Rnds 1 and 2 for half brioche stitch.

## Notes
1. Cardigan is worked flat, from the bottom up, beginning with a split hem, then joined partway through half brioche and continued to pocket openings. Stitches are held for button bands while body is worked in reverse stockinette to underarm, then fronts and back are worked with short row shoulder shaping, and joined using the three-needle bind off. Stitches are picked up around armhole edge and worked in the round to cuff. Button bands are worked in half brioche stitch and sewn to fronts. Stitches are picked up along neck edge and worked in a half brioche trim.
2. Buttonholes are worked using markers placed on button band as a guide. Work a few buttons at the top, or place buttons all the way to the pocket line. The top button will be worked in the neck trim.

# cardigan

## Pocket lining (Make 2)

With largest circular needle (circ), or if you prefer, work back and forth on two double-pointed needles (dpns), using the long-tail cast on, CO 23 sts.

**First row:** (RS) Purl.

**Next row:** Knit.

Cont in rev St st for 5¼" [13.5 cm], ending after a RS (purl) row.

**Next row:** (WS) BO 1 st, knit to end.

**Next row:** BO 1 st, purl to end—21 sts rem.

Break yarn. Place sts onto waste yarn.

## Back

With middle-sized circ and using the long-tail cast on, CO 77 (83, 89, 95, 101, 107, 113, 119) sts. Do not join.

## Begin half brioche

**First row:** (RS) Work Row 1 of half brioche st to end.

**Next row:** Work next row of patt.

Cont in patt for 6" [15 cm], ending after a WS row.

Break yarn. Place sts onto waste yarn.

## Left front

With middle-sized circ and using the long-tail cast on, CO 43 (45, 49, 51, 55, 57, 61, 63) sts. Do not join.

## Begin half brioche trim

**First row:** (RS) Work Row 1 of half brioche st to end.

**Next row:** Work next row of patt.

Cont in patt for 4" [10 cm], ending after a WS row.

Break yarn. Place sts onto waste yarn.

## Right front

Work right front same as for left front. Do not break yarn.

## Join fronts and back

**Next row** *dec row:* (RS) With RS of all pcs facing and yarn attached at right front, sl 1, (k1, sl1yo) to last 2 right front sts, k1, sl next st to RH needle, return sts for back to LH needle, return sl st to LH needle and p2tog with first back st, place marker for side (pm), (k1, sl1yo) to last 2 back sts, k1, pm for side, sl next st to RH needle, return sts for left front to LH needle, return sl st to LH needle and p2tog with first left front st, (k1, sl1yo) to last 2 sts, k2 (2 sts dec'd)—161 (171, 185, 195, 209, 219, 233, 243) sts on needle; 43 (45, 49, 51, 55, 57, 61, 63) sts for each front and 75 (81, 87, 93, 99, 105, 111, 117) for back.

**Next row:** (WS) Sl 1, p1, (brk, p1) to 1 st before marker (m), k1, slip marker (sl m), p1, (brk, p1) to m, p1, sl m, k1, p1, (brk, p1) to last st, k1.

**Next row:** Work Row 1 of half brioche st to end.

Cont in patt until back meas 9" [23 cm] from beg, ending after a WS row.

Change to largest circ.

## Begin pocket set up and hold stitches for button bands

*Note:* This RS row is knitted to finish brioche pattern.

**Next row:** (RS) Work as est for 7 sts, then place these sts onto waste yarn, using the cable cast on, CO 1 st, k8 (10, 12, 14, 16, 18, 20, 22), then BO the next 21 sts in p1, k1 rib, knit to last 35 (37, 39, 41, 43, 45, 47, 49) sts, BO next 21 sts in p1, k1 rib, k7 (9, 11, 13, 15, 17, 19, 21), then sl rem 7 sts onto waste yarn, turn work, CO 1 st.

## Begin reverse stockinette and join pockets

**Next row:** (WS) With WS of all pcs facing, *knit to pocket opening, place pocket sts onto LH needle, then knit across; rep from * one more time, knit to end—149 (159, 173, 183, 197, 207, 221, 231) sts on needle.

**Next row:** Purl.

Cont in rev St st until back meas 16" [40.5 cm] from beg, ending after a WS (knit) row.

## Begin underarm shaping

**Next row** *inc row:* (RS) Purl to 1 st before m, m1-p, p1, sl m, m1-p, purl to next m, m1-p, sl m, p1, m1-p, purl to end (4 sts inc'd)—153 (163, 177, 187, 201, 211, 225, 235) sts.

Rep *inc row* every 4 rows one more time, then every RS row two times—165 (175, 189, 199, 213, 223, 237, 247) sts.

**Next row** *inc row:* (WS) Knit to m, sl m, k1-f/b, knit to 1 st before next m, k1-f/b, sl m, knit to end (2 sts inc'd in back)—167 (177, 191, 201, 215, 225, 239, 249) sts; 41 (43, 47, 49, 53, 55, 59, 61) sts for each front and 85 (91, 97, 103, 109, 115, 121, 127) for back.

## Separate fronts and back

**Next row:** (RS) Purl to side m, place sts to next side m onto waste yarn for back, then place rem sts for for left front onto separate waste yarn, purl to end—41 (43, 47, 49, 53, 55, 59, 61) sts on needle for right front.

## Right front

**Next row:** (WS) Using the cable cast on, CO 5 sts, knit to end—46 (48, 52, 54, 58, 60, 64, 66) sts.

**Next row:** Purl.

Cont in rev St st until pc meas 5¼ (5½, 6, 6¼, 6¾, 7¼, 7½, 8)" [13.5 (14, 15, 16, 17, 18.5, 19, 20.5) cm] from underarm, ending after a RS row.

## Begin shoulder and neck shaping

Do not count yarnovers as stitches.

**Next row** *short row 1:* (WS) Knit to end; (RS) BO 3 (3, 4, 4, 5, 5, 6, 6) sts, purl to last 3 (4, 4, 5, 5, 5, 6, 6) sts, turn—43 (45, 48, 50, 53, 55, 58, 60) sts rem.

**Next row** *short row 2:* (WS) Yo, knit to end; (RS) BO 2 sts, purl to 3 (3, 4, 4, 4, 4, 5, 5) sts before last gap, turn—41 (43, 46, 48, 51, 53, 56, 58) sts rem.

**Next row** *short row 3:* (WS) Yo, knit to end; (RS) BO 1 st, purl to 3 (3, 4, 4, 4, 5, 5, 5) sts before last gap, turn—40 (42, 45, 47, 50, 52, 55, 57) sts rem.

**Next row** *short row 4:* (WS) Yo, knit to end; (RS) BO 1 st, purl to 3 (4, 4, 4, 4, 5, 5, 5) sts before last gap, turn—39 (41, 44, 46, 49, 51, 54, 56) sts rem.

**Next row** *short row 5:* (WS) Yo, knit to end; (RS) BO 1 st, purl to 4 (4, 4, 4, 5, 5, 5, 5) sts before last gap, turn—38 (40, 43, 45, 48, 50, 53, 55) sts rem.

**Next row** *short row 6:* Rep *short row 5*— 37 (39, 42, 44, 47, 49, 52, 54) sts rem.

**Next row** *short row 7:* (WS) Yo, knit to end; (RS) purl to 4 (4, 4, 4, 5, 5, 5, 6) sts before last gap, turn.

**Next row** *short row 8:* (WS) Yo, knit to end; (RS) purl to 4 (4, 4, 5, 5, 5, 5, 6) sts before last gap, turn.

**Next row** *short row 9:* (WS) Yo, knit to end; (RS) purl to 4 (4, 5, 5, 5, 5, 6, 6) sts before last gap, turn.

**Next row:** (WS) Yo, knit to end.

**Next row:** Purl to end, p2tog each yo with the st after gap.

Break yarn leaving a long tail for finishing. Place sts onto waste yarn.

## Left front

Return sts for left front to larger circ. Join yarn ready to work a RS row.

**Next row:** (RS) Using the cable cast on, CO 5 sts, purl to end—46 (48, 52, 54, 58, 60, 64, 66) sts on needle.

**Next row:** Knit.

Cont in rev St st until pc meas 5¼ (5½, 6, 6¼, 6¾, 7¼, 7½, 8)" [13.5 (14, 15, 16, 17, 18.5, 19, 20.5) cm] from underarm, ending after a RS row.

## Begin shoulder and neck shaping

Do not count yarnovers as stitches.

**Next row** *short row 1:* (WS) BO 3 (3, 4, 4, 5, 5, 6, 6) sts, knit to last 3 (4, 4, 5, 5, 5, 6, 6) sts, turn; (RS) yo, purl to end—43 (45, 48, 50, 53, 55, 58, 60) sts rem.

**Next row** *short row 2:* (WS) BO 2 sts, knit to 3 (3, 4, 4, 4, 4, 5, 5) sts before last gap, turn; (RS) yo, purl to end—41 (43, 46, 48, 51, 53, 56, 58) sts rem.

**Next row** *short row 3:* (WS) BO 1 st, knit to 3 (3, 4, 4, 4, 5, 5, 5) sts before last gap, turn; (RS) yo, purl to end—40 (42, 45, 47, 50, 52, 55, 57) sts rem.

**Next row** *short row 4:* (WS) BO 1 st, knit to 3 (4, 4, 4, 4, 5, 5, 5) sts before last gap, turn; (RS) yo, purl to end—39 (41, 44, 46, 49, 51, 54, 56) sts rem.

**Next row** *short row 5:* (WS) BO 1 st, knit to 4 (4, 4, 4, 5, 5, 5, 5) sts before last gap, turn; (RS) yo, purl to end—38 (40, 43, 45, 48, 50, 53, 55) sts rem.

**Next row** *short row 6:* Rep *short row 5*— 37 (39, 42, 44, 47, 49, 52, 54) sts rem.

**Next row** *short row 7:* (WS) Knit to 4 (4, 4, 4, 5, 5, 5, 6) sts before last gap, turn; (RS) yo, purl to end.

**Next row** *short row 8:* (WS) Knit to 4 (4, 4, 5, 5, 5, 5, 6) sts before last gap, turn; (RS) yo, purl to end.

**Next row** *short row 9:* (WS) Knit to 4 (4, 5, 5, 5, 5, 6, 6) sts before last gap, turn; (RS) yo, purl to end.

**Next row:** (WS) Knit to end, ssk each yo with the st after gap.

**Next row:** Purl.

Break yarn. Place sts onto waste yarn.

## Back

Return sts for back to larger circ.

**Next row:** (RS) With RS of back facing and beg at right armhole edge, pick up and knit 5 sts in underarm CO from right front, purl across back sts, then pick up and knit 5 sts in underarm CO from left front—95 (101, 107, 113, 119, 125, 131, 137) sts on needle.

**Next row:** Knit.

Cont in rev St st until pc meas 5¼ (5½, 6, 6¼, 6¾, 7¼, 7½, 8)" [13.5 (14, 15, 16, 17, 18.5, 19, 20.5) cm] from underarm, ending after a WS row.

**Next row** *place markers:* (RS) P42 (44, 47, 49, 52, 54, 57, 59), pm for neck, p11 (13, 13, 15, 15, 17, 17, 19), pm for neck, p42 (44, 47, 49, 52, 54, 57, 59) sts to end.

## Begin shoulder shaping

**Next row** *short row 1:* (WS) Knit to last 3 (4, 4, 5, 5, 5, 6, 6) sts, turn; (RS) yo, purl to last 3 (4, 4, 5, 5, 5, 6, 6) sts, turn.

**Next row** *short row 2:* (WS) Yo, knit to 3 (3, 4, 4, 4, 4, 5, 5) sts before last gap, turn; (RS) yo, purl to 3 (3, 4, 4, 4, 4, 5, 5) sts before last gap, turn.

**Next row** *short row 3:* (WS) Yo, knit to 3 (3, 4, 4, 5, 5, 5) sts before last gap, turn; (RS) yo, purl to 3 (3, 4, 4, 4, 5, 5, 5) sts before last gap, turn.

**Next row** *short row 4:* (WS) Yo, knit to 3 (4, 4, 4, 5, 5, 5) sts before last gap, turn; (RS) yo, purl to 3 (4, 4, 4, 4, 5, 5, 5) sts before last gap, turn.

**Next row** *short row 5:* (WS) Yo, knit to 4 (4, 4, 4, 5, 5, 5, 5) sts before last gap, turn; (RS) yo, purl to 4 (4, 4, 4, 5, 5, 5, 5) sts before last gap, turn.

**Next row** *short row 6:* Rep *short row 5.*

## Begin neck and continue shoulder shaping

**Next row** *short row 7:* (WS) Yo, knit to m, join a new ball of yarn and BO all sts to next m, removing marker to BO last st, knit to 4 (4, 4, 4, 5, 5, 5, 6) sts before last gap, turn; (RS) yo, purl to right neck edge; on left neck edge, purl to 4 (4, 4, 4, 5, 5, 5, 6) sts before last gap, turn—42 (44, 47, 49, 52, 54, 57, 59) sts rem for each side.

**Next row** *short row 8:* (WS) Yo, knit to neck edge; then BO 3 sts, knit to 4 (4, 4, 5, 5, 5, 5, 6) sts before last gap, turn; (RS) yo, purl to neck edge; then BO 3 sts, purl to 4 (4, 4, 5, 5, 5, 5, 6) sts before last gap, turn—39 (41, 44, 46, 49, 51, 54, 56) sts rem each.

**Next row** *short row 9:* (WS) Yo, knit to neck edge; then BO 2 sts, knit to 4 (4, 5, 5, 5, 6, 6) sts before last gap, turn; (RS) yo, purl to neck edge; then BO 2 sts, purl to 4 (4, 5, 5, 5, 5, 6, 6) sts before last gap, turn—37 (39, 42, 44, 47, 49, 52, 54) sts rem each.

**Next row:** (WS) Yo, knit to neck edge; then knit to end, ssk each yo with the st after gap.

**Next row:** (RS) With yarn attached at left neck edge, purl to end, p2tog each yo with the st after gap.

Break yarn at neck edge only.

## Join shoulders

Place sts for front shoulders onto smaller circ. With WS (knit) of pcs tog, largest needle, and attached yarn, using the three-needle bind off, BO all sts for left shoulder. With yarn attached at right armhole edge, rep for right shoulder.

Gently steam block piece.

## Sleeves

With RS facing and larger dpns, beg at underarm, pick up and knit 24 (25, 26, 28, 30, 32, 33, 35) sts along armhole edge to shoulder seam (approx 2 sts for every 3 rows), then pick up and knit 24 (25, 26, 28, 30, 32, 33, 35) sts to underarm—48 (50, 52, 56, 60, 64, 66, 70) sts on needles. Pm for beg of rnd.

**First rnd:** Purl.

Cont in rev St st until sleeve meas 1" [2.5 cm] from pick-up.

## Begin sleeve shaping

**Next rnd** *dec rnd:* P2, p2tog, purl to last 4 sts, p2tog, p2 (2 sts dec'd)—46 (48, 50, 54, 58, 62, 64, 68) sts rem.

Rep *dec rnd* every 10 (8, 8, 8, 6, 6, 6, 6) rnds 3 (6, 3, 1, 8, 3, 3, 2) more times, then every 8 (6, 6, 6, 4, 4, 4, 4) rnds 3 (1, 5, 8, 2, 9, 9, 11) times—34 (34, 34, 36, 38, 38, 40, 42) sts rem.

Cont in rev St st until sleeve meas 11" [28 cm] from pick-up.

**Next rnd:** Knit.

Change to smaller dpns.

## Begin cuff trim

**Next rnd:** Work Rnd 1 of half brioche st to end.

**Next rnd:** Work next rnd of patt.

Cont in patt for 7" [18 cm], ending after Rnd 2.

**Next rnd:** Bind off in k1, p1 rib.

## Finishing

Weave in ends. Wet block cardigan to finished measurements.

## Button band

Place sts held for right front band onto middle-sized circ or dpn. Join yarn ready to work a WS row.

**Next row:** (WS) Using the cable cast on, CO 1 st, k1, (brk, p1) three times, k1—8 sts.

**Next row:** Sl 1, (k1, sl1yo) three times, k1.

Cont as est until band meas same length as body from beg of rev St st, ending after a RS row.

Do not break yarn. Place sts onto waste yarn.

Sew band to right front using the mattress stitch.

Measure 2¼" [5.5 cm] down from stitches on waste yarn and place a locking st marker into a stitch on the band. Measure 3½" [9 cm] down from first marker and place another. Rep for desired number of buttons (sample shown with four). These markers will be used as guides as you work the button band.

## Buttonhole band

Place sts held for left front band onto middle-sized circ or dpn. Join yarn ready to work a RS row.

**Next row:** (RS) Using the cable cast on, CO 1 st, k1, (sl1yo, k1) three times, k1.

**Next row:** Sl 1, (p1, brk) three times, k1.

Cont as est in half brioche and compare buttonhole band length to button band until you reach the lowest button marker, ending after a WS row.

**Next row** *buttonhole row 1:* (RS) K1, sl1yo, ssk, yo2, k1, sl1yo, k2.

**Next row** *buttonhole row 2:* (WS) Sl 1, p1, brk, p1, knit into yo dropping extra wrap, p1, brk, k1.

Buttonholes are worked with a double yarnover and fall within a purl trough so they are virtually invisible. Miraculously, a double yarnover seems to make a hole that always fits a button appropriate to the yarn weight.

Cont in patt, comparing length frequently to button band, and rep *buttonhole rows 1 and 2* at each marker, then cont in patt until buttonhole band meas same as button band, ending after a WS row.

Break yarn. Place sts onto waste yarn.

Sew band to left front using the mattress stitch.

## Neck trim

Place sts for right front band onto smallest circ. With RS facing and yarn attached at band, pick up and knit 1 st in each BO st and 2 sts for every 3 rows along neck edge, making sure to pick up an odd number of sts. With RS facing, place sts for left buttonhole band onto LH needle, then k1, (sl1yo, k1) three times, k1.

**First row** *dec row:* (WS) Sl 1, (p1, brk) three times, p2tog, *k1, p1; rep from * to last 10 sts, k1, p2tog, (brk, p1) three times, k1 (2 sts dec'd).

**Next row:** Work Row 1 of half brioche st to end. Cont in patt for 1" [2.5 cm], ending after a WS row.

**Next row** *buttonhole row 1:* (RS) Work in patt to last 6 sts, ssk, yo2, k1, sl1yo, k2.

**Next row** *buttonhole row 2:* (WS) Sl 1, p1, brk, p1, knit into yo dropping extra wrap, *p1, brk; rep from * to last 2 sts, p1, k1.

Cont in patt for 4 more rows.

**Next row:** (RS) Bind off in pattern.

Sew pocket linings to WS of fronts.

Sew buttons opposite buttonholes.

Weave in rem ends and block again, if you like.

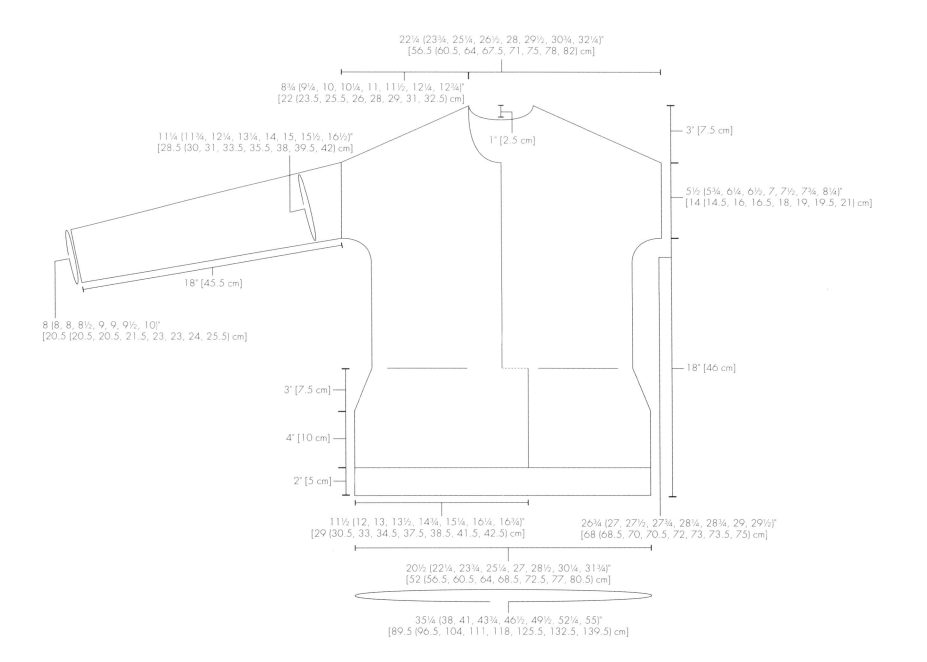

22¼ (23¾, 25¼, 26½, 28, 29½, 30¾, 32¼)"
[56.5 (60.5, 64, 67.5, 71, 75, 78, 82) cm]

8¾ (9¼, 10, 10¼, 11, 11½, 12¼, 12¾)"
[22 (23.5, 25.5, 26, 28, 29, 31, 32.5) cm]

11¼ (11¾, 12¼, 13¼, 14, 15, 15½, 16½)"
[28.5 (30, 31, 33.5, 35.5, 38, 39.5, 42) cm]

1" [2.5 cm]

3" [7.5 cm]

5½ (5¾, 6¼, 6½, 7, 7½, 7¾, 8¼)"
[14 (14.5, 16, 16.5, 18, 19, 19.5, 21) cm]

18" [45.5 cm]

8 (8, 8, 8½, 9, 9, 9½, 10)"
[20.5 (20.5, 20.5, 21.5, 23, 23, 24, 25.5) cm]

18" [46 cm]

3" [7.5 cm]

4" [10 cm]

2" [5 cm]

11½ (12, 13, 13½, 14¾, 15¼, 16¼, 16¾)"
[29 (30.5, 33, 34.5, 37.5, 38.5, 41.5, 42.5) cm]

26¾ (27, 27½, 27¾, 28¼, 28¾, 29, 29½)"
[68 (68.5, 70, 70.5, 72, 73, 73.5, 75) cm]

20½ (22¼, 23¾, 25¼, 27, 28½, 30¼, 31¾)"
[52 (56.5, 60.5, 64, 68.5, 72.5, 77, 80.5) cm]

35¼ (38, 41, 43¾, 46½, 49½, 52¼, 55)"
[89.5 (96.5, 104, 111, 118, 125.5, 132.5, 139.5) cm]

# maple

This little cardigan is as brief as you can get. That said, there are a few things worth pointing out. For example, the back neck here is narrow, which allows the collar to hug the neck a bit. Also, the wide front borders are worked in a plush variation of brioche stitch and without buttons to close it, the strong, uninterrupted vertical lines catch the eye. Finally, the sleeves are slim, and extra long cuffs hug and cover the wrists.

## Finished measurements
36 (40½, 45, 49¼, 53¾, 58¼, 62¾)" [91.5 (103, 114.5, 125, 136.5, 148, 159.5) cm] bust circumference; shown in size 40½" [103 cm] on a 32" [81 cm], 5'10" [178 cm] tall model (8½" [21.5 cm] positive ease)

## Yarn
Owl by Quince & Co
(50% American wool, 50% alpaca; 120yd [110m]/50g)
- 8 (8, 9, 10, 11, 12, 13) skeins Barred 307

## Needles
- One 32" circular needle (circ) in size US 8 [5 mm]
- One 32" circ in size US 7 [4.5 mm]
- One set double-pointed needles (dpns) in size US 8 [5 mm]
- One set dpns in size US 7 [4.5 mm]

Or size to obtain gauge

## Notions
- Stitch markers
- Waste yarn
- Tapestry needle

## Gauge
18 sts and 26 rows = 4" [10 cm] in stockinette stitch with larger needles, after wet blocking
16 sts and 34 rows = 4" [10 cm] in half brioche stitch with larger needles, after wet blocking

## Special abbreviation
sl 1: Slip 1 st knitwise with yarn in back.

## Half brioche stitch (odd number of stitches)
Row 1: (RS) *K1, sl1yo; rep from * to last st, k1.
Row 2: *P1, brk; rep from * to last st, p1.
Repeat Rows 1 and 2 for half brioche stitch.

## Note
Cardi is knitted flat, from the bottom up, in one piece to underarm. Fronts and back are worked to shoulders with short row shaping, then joined using the three-needle bind off. Stitches at neck edge are continued then joined and sewn to create back neck edge. Stitches are picked up around armhole edge and knitted in the round to cuff.

Maple is worked primarily in stockinette stitch with knitted-at-the-same-time front borders, which means—good news—there's nothing more to pick up and knit when you bind off. And herein lies the design conundrum. The row gauge for stockinette stitch and that for brioche stitch are quite different. Brioche requires more rows per inch than stockinette. How to make the bands and the fronts the same length without knitting them separately and seaming them together?

Why, with short rows, of course. But no worries, short rows worked vertically along the column that separates body from border couldn't—simply COULDN'T—be easier. Trust me.

# cardi

With smaller circular needle (circ) and using the long-tail cast on, CO 161 (181, 201, 221, 241, 261, 281) sts. Do not join.

## Begin rib trim and front panels

**First row:** (RS) Sl 1, work Row 1 of half brioche st over next 21 sts, place marker for panel (pm), p1, *k1, p1; rep from * to last 22 sts, pm for panel, work Row 1 of half brioche st to last st, p1.

**Next row:** Sl 1, work next row of patt to marker (m), k1, *p1, k1; rep from * to next panel m, work next row of patt to last st, p1.

**Next row:** Sl 1, work in half brioche st to m, p1, *k1, p1; rep from * to next m, work in half brioche st to last st, p1.

Cont as est in rib and half brioche for 1½" [4 cm], ending after a WS row.

Change to larger circ.

## Begin stockinette and continue front panels

**Next row:** (RS) Sl 1, work in patt to m, knit to next m, work in patt to last st, p1.

**Next row:** Sl 1, work in patt to m, purl to next m, work in patt to last st, p1.

## Begin short row shaping

Short rows occur where the front panels of half brioche stitch meet with stockinette. They keep the front panels from becoming too short, due to the different row gauges of the patterns.

**Next row** short row 1: (RS) Work as est to panel m, k1, turn; (WS) yo, p1, work as est to end.

**Next row:** (RS) Work to panel m, k1, k2tog the yo with the st after gap, knit to next panel m, work to end.

**Next row** short row 2: (WS) Work to panel m, p1, turn; (RS) yo, k1, work to end.

**Next row:** (WS) Work to panel m, p1, ssp the yo with the st after gap, purl to next m, work to end.

Work 6 rows even in St st with front panels; 10 rows have been worked in stockinette, 12 rows in each front panel.

Rep the last 10 rows (beg from short row 1) three more times, then work short rows 1 and 2 along with their pick-up rows one time.

Piece meas approx 8½" [21.5 cm] from beg, measured straight down at center back.

Work 1 RS row even.

**Next row** place markers: (WS) Work to panel m, p18 (23, 28, 33, 38, 43, 48), pm for side, p81 (91, 101, 111, 121, 131, 141), pm for side, p18 (23, 28, 33, 38, 43, 48) to next panel m, work to end.

## Begin side shaping

**Next row** inc row: (RS) *Work as est to 1 st before side m, M1R, k1, slip marker (sl m), k1, M1L; rep from * one more time, work as est to end (4 sts inc'd)—165 (185, 205, 225, 245, 265, 285) sts.

Work 3 rows even, then rep short row 1.

**Next row** inc row: (RS) Work to panel m, k1, k2tog the yo with the st after gap, *knit to 1 st before side m, M1R, k1, sl m, k1, M1L; rep from * one more time, knit to panel m, work to end—169 (189, 209, 229, 249, 269, 289) sts on needle; 42 (47, 52, 57, 62, 67, 72) sts for each front and 85 (95, 105, 115, 125, 135, 145) sts for back.

**Next row:** Rep short row 2.

**Next row:** Work to panel m, p1, ssp the yo with the st after gap, purl to next m, work to end.

## Separate fronts and back

**Next row:** (RS) Work as est to side m, place sts for back onto waste yarn, then place rem sts for left front onto separate waste yarn—42 (47, 52, 57, 62, 67, 72) sts on needle for right front.

## Right front

**Next row:** (WS) Using the cable cast on, CO 7 sts, purl to panel m, work in half brioche st to last st, p1—49 (54, 59, 64, 69, 74, 79) sts.

Cont in St st and half brioche for 4 more rows.

**Next row** front panel short row: (RS) Work to panel m, k1, turn; (WS) yo, p1, work to end.

**Next row:** (RS) Work to panel m, k1, k2tog the yo with the st after gap, knit to end.

Work 8 rows even in St st and half brioche.

Rep the last 10 rows (beg from front panel short row) and cont in St st and half brioche until pc meas 5½ (5¾, 6, 6½, 7, 7½, 8½)" [14 (14.5, 15, 16.5, 18, 19, 21.5) cm] from underarm, ending after a WS row.

## Begin shoulder shaping

Continue working *front panel short row* every 10 rows as established to end of shoulder shaping. Do not count yarnovers as stitches.

**Next row** *short row 1:* (RS) Work as est to last 5 (6, 6, 7, 7, 8, 8) sts, turn; (WS) yo, work to end.

**Next row** *short row 2:* (RS) Work to 3 (4, 4, 5, 5, 6, 6) sts before last gap, turn; (WS) yo, work to end.

Rep *short row two* 2 (4, 1, 3, 0, 2, 0) more times.

**Next row** *short row 3:* (RS) Work to 4 (5, 5, 6, 6, 7, 7) sts before last gap, turn; (WS) yo, work to end.

Rep *short row three* 0 (0, 1, 1, 2, 2, 1) more times.

**Next row** *short row 4:* (RS) Work to 5 (6, 6, 7, 7, 8, 8) sts before last gap, turn; (WS) yo, work to end.

Rep *short row four* 3 (1, 3, 1, 3, 1, 4) more times.

**Next row:** (RS) Work to end, working each yo tog with the st after gap as follows: k2tog if a knit st and p2tog if the st is meant to be a sl1yo.

**Next row:** Work to end.

**Next row:** Work 10 sts, then using the backward loop cast on, CO 1 st, place rem 39 (44, 49, 54, 59, 64, 69) sts onto waste yarn—11 sts on needle.

## Begin neck trim

Change to larger double-pointed needles (dpns), if you like.

**Next row:** (WS) K1, work in patt to end.

**Next row:** Work in patt to last st, k1.

Cont as est for 2¾" [7 cm], ending after a WS row.

Break yarn. Place sts onto waste yarn.

## Left front

Return sts held for left front to larger circ, ready to work a RS row.

**Next row:** (RS) Using the cable cast on, CO 7 sts, knit to m, work in half brioche st to last st, p1—49 (54, 59, 64, 69, 74, 79) sts on needle.

**Next row:** Work to panel m, knit to end.

Work 5 more rows in St st and half brioche.

**Next row** *front panel short row:* (WS) Work to panel m, p1, turn; (RS) yo, k1, work to end.
**Next row:** (WS) Work to panel m, p1, ssp the yo with the st after gap, purl to end.
Work 8 rows even in St st and half brioche.
Rep the last 10 rows (beg from *front panel short row*) and cont in St st and half brioche until pc meas 5½ (5¾, 6, 6½, 7, 7½, 8½)" [14 (14.5, 15, 16.5, 18, 19, 21.5) cm] from underarm, ending after a WS row.

## Begin shoulder shaping
Continue working *front panel short row* every 10 rows as established to end of shoulder shaping. Do not count yarnovers as stitches.
**Next row** *short row 1:* (RS) Work as est to end; (WS) work to last 5 (6, 6, 7, 7, 8, 8) sts, turn.
**Next row** *short row 2:* (RS) Yo, work to end; (WS) work to 3 (4, 4, 5, 5, 6, 6) sts before last gap, turn.
Rep *short row two* 2 (4, 1, 3, 0, 2, 0) more times.
**Next row** *short row 3:* (RS) Yo, work to end; (WS) work to 4 (5, 5, 6, 6, 7, 7) sts before last gap, turn.
Rep *short row three* 0 (0, 1, 1, 2, 2, 1) more times.
**Next row** *short row 4:* (RS) Yo, work to end; (WS) work to 5 (6, 6, 7, 7, 8, 8) sts before last gap, turn.
Rep *short row four* 3 (1, 3, 1, 3, 1, 4) more times.
**Next row:** (RS) Yo, work to end.

**Next row:** Work 10 sts, using the backward loop cast on, CO 1 st, then work to end, working each yo tog with the st after gap as follows: ssp if a purl st and br-ssk if the st is meant to be a brk.
Break yarn. Place last 39 (44, 49, 54, 59, 64, 69) sts onto waste yarn—11 sts rem for trim.

## Begin neck trim
Change to larger dpns, if you like.
Join yarn ready to work a RS row.
**Next row:** (RS) K1, work in patt to end.
**Next row:** Work in patt to last st, k1.
Cont as est for 2¾" [7 cm], ending after a WS row.
Break yarn. Place sts onto waste yarn.

## Back
Return sts for back to larger circ.
**Next row:** (RS) With RS of back facing and beg at right armhole edge, pick up and knit 7 sts in underarm CO from right front, knit across back sts, then pick up and knit 7 sts in underarm CO from left front—99 (109, 119, 129, 139, 149, 159) sts on needle.
**Next row:** Purl.
Cont in St st until pc meas 5½ (5¾, 6, 6½, 7, 7½, 8½)" [14 (14.5, 15, 16.5, 18, 19, 21.5) cm] from underarm, ending after a RS row.
**Next row** *place markers:* (WS) P39 (44, 49, 54, 59, 64, 69), pm for neck, p21, pm for neck, p39 (44, 49, 54, 59, 64, 69) sts to end.

## Begin shoulder shaping
**Next row** *short row 1:* (RS) Knit to last 5 (6, 6, 7, 7, 8, 8) sts, turn; (WS) yo, purl to last 5 (6, 6, 7, 7, 8, 8) sts, turn.
**Next row** *short row 2:* (RS) Yo, knit to 3 (4, 4, 5, 5, 6, 6) sts before last gap, turn; (WS) yo, purl to 3 (4, 4, 5, 5, 6, 6) sts before last gap, turn.
Rep *short row two* 2 (4, 1, 3, 0, 2, 0) more times.
**Next row** *short row 3:* (RS) Yo, knit to 4 (5, 5, 6, 6, 7, 7) sts before last gap, turn; (WS) yo, purl to 4 (5, 5, 6, 6, 7, 7) sts before last gap, turn.
Rep *short row three* 0 (0, 1, 1, 2, 2, 1) more times.
**Next row** *short row 4:* (RS) Yo, knit to 5 (6, 6, 7, 7, 8, 8) sts before last gap, turn; (WS) yo, purl to 5 (6, 6, 7, 7, 8, 8) sts before last gap, turn.
Rep *short row four* 3 (1, 3, 1, 3, 1, 4) more times.
**Next row:** (RS) Yo, knit to end, k2tog each yo with the st after gap.
**Next row:** Purl to end, ssp each yo with the st after gap.

## Join shoulders
Place sts for front shoulders onto smaller circ. With RS of pcs tog and attached yarn, using the three-needle bind off, BO all right front sts with corresponding back sts to first m, BO back neck sts to next m, then BO rem back sts with corresponding left front sts.

Gently steam block piece.

## Sleeves

With RS facing and larger dpns, beg at underarm, pick up and knit 28 (29, 30, 33, 35, 37, 42) sts along armhole edge to shoulder seam (approx 2 sts for every 3 rows), then pick up and knit 28 (29, 30, 33, 35, 37, 42) sts to underarm—56 (58, 60, 66, 70, 74, 84) sts on needles. Pm for beg of rnd.

**First rnd:** Knit.

Cont in St st for 8 (6, 6, 4, 4, 4, 2) more rnds.

## Begin sleeve shaping

**Next rnd** *dec rnd:* K1, k2tog, knit to last 3 sts, ssk, k1 (2 sts dec'd)—54 (56, 58, 64, 68, 72, 82) sts rem.

Rep *dec rnd* every 10 (8, 8, 8, 6, 6, 4) rnds 3 (7, 7, 1, 9, 7, 16) more times, then every 8 (0, 0, 6, 4, 4, 0) rnds 3 (0, 0, 9, 2, 5, 0) times—42 (42, 44, 44, 46, 48, 50) sts rem.

Cont in St st until sleeve meas 11" [28 cm] from pick-up.

Change to smaller dpns.

## Begin cuff trim

**Next rnd:** *K1, p1; rep from * to end.

Cont in rib for 4" [10 cm].

**Next rnd:** Bind off in pattern.

## Finishing

Weave in ends. Wet block cardi to finished measurements.

Return sts held for right and left neck trim to 2 dpns. With RS of pcs tog, using the three-needle bind off, BO all sts.

Sew side edge of neck trim to back neck.

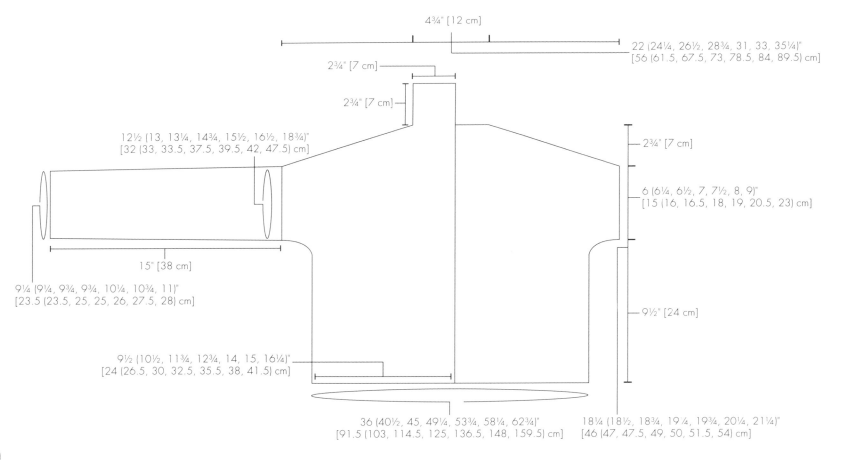

4¾" [12 cm]

22 (24¼, 26½, 28¾, 31, 33, 35¼)" [56 (61.5, 67.5, 73, 78.5, 84, 89.5) cm]

2¾" [7 cm]

2¾" [7 cm]

12½ (13, 13¼, 14¾, 15½, 16½, 18¾)" [32 (33, 33.5, 37.5, 39.5, 42, 47.5) cm]

2¾" [7 cm]

6 (6¼, 6½, 7, 7½, 8, 9)" [15 (16, 16.5, 18, 19, 20.5, 23) cm]

15" [38 cm]

9¼ (9¼, 9¾, 9¾, 10¼, 10¾, 11)" [23.5 (23.5, 25, 25, 26, 27.5, 28) cm]

9½" [24 cm]

9½ (10½, 11¾, 12¾, 14, 15, 16¼)" [24 (26.5, 30, 32.5, 35.5, 38, 41.5) cm]

36 (40½, 45, 49¼, 53¾, 58¼, 62¾)" [91.5 (103, 114.5, 125, 136.5, 148, 159.5) cm]

18¼ (18½, 18¾, 19 ¼, 19¾, 20¼, 21¼)" [46 (47, 47.5, 49, 50, 51.5, 54) cm]

# balsam

A hoodie all on its own, Balsam is warm and snuggly around neck and ears. Pull it on, tuck your chin in, and you're good to go. Cushy brioche-rib panels cover front and back, then knit in stockinette stitch to form a cowl deep enough to stretch up and over the head for a soft hood.

## Finished measurements
28" [71 cm] circumference at top and 23" [58.5 cm] tall

## Yarn
Owl by Quince & Co
(50% American wool, 50% alpaca; 120yd [110m]/50g)
- 5 skeins Taiga 328

## Needles
- One 24" circular needle (circ) in size US 8 [5 mm]
- One 24" circ in size US 7 [4.5 mm]

Or size to obtain gauge

## Gauge
14 sts and 46 rows = 4" [10 cm] in brioche stitch with smaller needles, after wet blocking
16 sts and 23 rnds = 4" [10 cm] in stockinette stitch with larger needles, after wet blocking.

## Special abbreviation
sl 1: Slip 1 stitch purlwise with yarn in back.

## Brioche stitch (even number of stitches)
Set up row: (WS) Sl 1, *sl1yo, p1; rep from * to last st, k1.
Row 1: Sl 1, *sl1yo, brk; rep from * to last st, k1.
Repeat Row 1 every row for brioche stitch.

## Note
Cowl is knitted from the bottom up, beginning with front and back worked separately in brioche stitch, then joined in the round and continued in stockinette. Top of cowl is shaped using short rows. Side shaping begins in brioche and continues to beginning of short row shaping.

# cowl

With smaller circular needle (circ) and using the long-tail cast on, CO 62 sts. Do not join.

## Begin front trim
First row: (RS) Work set up row of brioche st to end.
Next row: Work Row 1 of patt.
Cont in patt for 5" [12.5 cm], ending after a WS row.
Next row dec row: (RS) Sl 1, sl1yo, brk, sl1yo, br-k3tog, sl1yo, *brk, sl1yo; rep from * to last 6 sts, br-sssk, sl1yo, brk, k1 (4 sts dec'd)—58 sts rem.
Work even in brioche st until pc meas 7½" [19 cm] from beg, ending after a WS row.
Change to larger circ.
Next row inc row: (RS) K8, *yo, k6; rep from * to last 2 sts, k2 (8 sts inc'd)—66 sts.
Break yarn. Place sts onto waste yarn.

---

In brioche stitch, the slant of shaping stitches, i.e. decreases and increases, stand out, one of the several things I especially like in this stitch pattern. To keep the rib consistent above the decrease, you work a double decrease (or increase). Note the decrease here just a few stitches in from the side edge.

A few short rows shape the hood to follow the curve of the back of the head.

## Begin back trim

With smaller circ and using the long-tail cast on, CO 62 sts. Do not join.

Work back trim same as for front, but leave on needles with yarn attached.

## Join front and back

**Next row:** With RS of both pcs facing and back trim at RH needle tip, return sts for front to LH needle, place marker (pm) for beg of rnd (BOR), knit across front sts, knitting each yo through the back loop, pm for side, knit across back sts, knitting each yo though the back loop—132 sts on needle. BOR counts as second side marker.

**Next rnd:** Knit.

Cont in St st for 14 more rnds.

## Begin side shaping

**Next rnd** *dec rnd:* *K2, k2tog, knit to 4 sts before side marker (m), ssk, k2; rep from * one more time (4 sts dec'd)—128 sts rem.

Rep *dec rnd* every 16 rnds one more time, then every 14 rnds three times—112 sts rem.

Piece meas approx 20½" [52 cm] from beg.

## Begin short row shaping

Do not count yarnovers as stitches.

**Next row** *short row 1:* (RS) K23, turn; (WS) yo, purl to BOR, purl across back to side m, p23, turn.

**Next row** *short row 2:* (RS) Yo, knit to 4 sts before last gap, turn; (WS) yo, purl to 4 sts before last gap, turn.

Rep *short row 2* five more times.

Last short row occurs 1 st before each side marker.

**Next row:** (RS) Yo, knit to BOR.

## Continue in the round

**Next rnd:** Knit to end, k2tog each yo with the st after gap for the first 7 short rows, then ssk each yo with the st before gap for rem 7 short rows.

**Next rnd:** Bind off loosely knitwise.

## Finishing

Weave in ends. Wet block cowl to finished measurements.

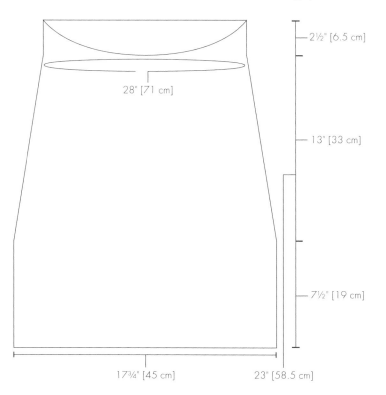

28" [71 cm]

2½" [6.5 cm]

13" [33 cm]

7½" [19 cm]

17¾" [45 cm]     23" [58.5 cm]

# shadbush

Stripes and a pom pom.
What more is there to say?

## Finished measurements
20" [51 cm] circumference and 10" [25.5 cm] tall
## Yarn
Owl by Quince & Co
(50% American wool, 50% alpaca; 120yd [110m]/50g)
- 1 skein Togian 333 (MC)
- 1 skein Snowy 300 (CC)
## Needles
- One 16" circular needle (circ) in size US 8 [5 mm]
- One 16" circ in size US 9 [5.5 mm]
- One set double-pointed needles in size US 9 [5.5 mm]
## Or size to obtain gauge
## Notions
- Stitch marker
- Tapestry needle
- Pom pom maker (optional)
## Gauge
16 sts and 24 rnds = 4" [10 cm] in stockinette stitch with larger needles, after wet blocking.

# hat

With MC and smaller circular needle (circ), using the long-tail cast on, CO 80 sts. Place marker for beg of rnd and join to work in the rnd, careful not to twist sts.

### Begin stockinette
**First rnd:** Knit.
With MC, knit 3 more rnds.
Change to larger circ.

### Begin stripes
**Next rnd:** With CC, knit to end.
**Next rnd:** With MC, knit to end.
Cont in stripes until hat meas 6½" [16.5 cm] from beg. Break MC.

### Continue in stockinette
**Next rnd:** With CC, knit to end.
Cont in St st until hat meas 9½" [24 cm] from beg.

### Begin crown shaping
Change to double-pointed needles when necessary.
**Next rnd:** *K2tog; rep from * to end (40 sts dec'd)—40 sts rem.
**Next rnd:** Knit.
**Next rnd:** Rep *dec rnd*—20 sts rem.
Break yarn and draw through rem sts.

### Finishing
Weave in ends. Wet block hat to finished measurements.

### Make pom
With MC and CC held tog, using your preferred method, make a 2-3" [5-7.5 cm] pom and sew to top of hat.

# stitches & techniques

## stockinette stitch (St st)
*Flat*
Knit on the RS, purl on the WS.
*In the round*
Knit every round.

## reverse stockinette stitch (rev St st)
*Flat*
Purl on the RS, knit on the WS.
*In the round*
Purl every round.

For great illustrated tutorials on the following techniques, visit our blog, quinceandco.com/blogs/news/tagged/techniques

backward loop cast on

cable cast on

basic bind off

three-needle bind off

cabling without a cable needle

mattress stitch

seaming

## making a slipknot

If beginning a long-tail cast on, from the tail end of your yarn ball, measure out about an inch for every stitch you'll cast on, and a few extra inches for good measure.
If working another type of cast on, a 6-8" [15-20 cm] tail will suffice.
At this point on your strand, make your first stitch, a slipknot, to secure the yarn to the needle.

Pull it through the loop.

Make a smallish loop, about the size of a silver dollar, overlapping the tail end on the working yarn.

Holding the loop just pulled through, pull gently on the yarn ends until the pulled-loop shrinks a little. This is your slipknot.

Reach through the loop and grab the tail.

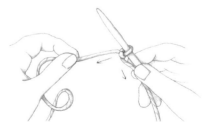

Put the slipknot on your needle. Snug the knot by gently pulling on both ends.

## long-tail cast on

Begin the long-tail cast on by making a slipknot.

Take a look at the strands hanging from the slipknot snugged on your needle. The working yarn is the end that comes from your ball.

Position the strands so the working yarn is on the right and the tail is on the left.

Hold the needle and the working yarn in your right hand, the tail in your left, a few inches away from the needle, with a little tension on it and thumb on top of yarn.

Create a loop by rotating your thumb under the tail end from behind, then up so your thumb is parallel with the needle and the yarn is looped around it.

Insert the tip of the needle upward into the loop formed around your thumb.

Secure this position by switching the needle to your left hand while it's still in the loop on your thumb and, with your right hand, wrap the working yarn counter-clockwise around the needle and sandwich it between the thumb and the needle in your left hand.

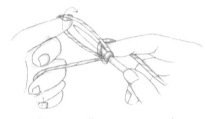

Now, grasp the needle again with your right hand and with your thumb lift the loop of yarn that's been sitting on it, bring it up and back and over the tip of the needle.

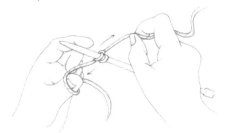

Repeat until you have cast on the number of stitches you need (remember: the slipknot counts as your first stitch).

## yarnover short rows

*In stockinette stitch*
On the right side, knit to the point where the short row begins. Turn work.

With the wrong side now facing, bring yarn to the back between needles and purl the next stitch so that yarn travels up and over the RH needle, creating a yarnover beside the stitch just worked. You are now ready to purl back along your short row.

On the wrong side, purl to the point where the short row begins. Turn work.

With the right side now facing, bring yarn to the front between needles and knit the next stitch so that the yarn travels up and over the RH needle, creating a yarnover beside the stitch just worked. You are now ready to knit back along your short row.

Continue working short rows as specified in your pattern.

After completing your short rows, each yarnover made at a turn is decreased with the stitch that follows the gap created by the turn.

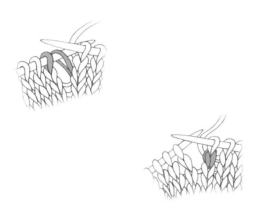

On the right side, knit to the yarnover, then k2tog the yarnover with the stitch after gap. Repeat for each yarnover as you work to the end of the row.

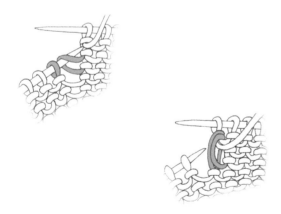

On the wrong side, purl to the yarnover, then ssp the yarnover with the stitch after gap. Repeat for each yarnover as you work to the end of the row.

*In reverse stockinette stitch*
The reverse stockinette patterns in this book begin short rows on the wrong side, so you will always be knitting first, turning work and purling, just like for stockinette.

After completing short rows, each yarnover is decreased with the stitch that follows the gap created by each turn so that the short rows are invisible on the purl side instead of the knit.

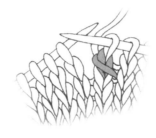

On the wrong (knit) side, knit to the yarnover, then ssk the yarnover with the stitch after gap. Repeat for each yarnover as you work to the end of the row.

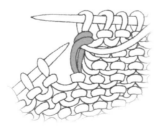

On the right (purl) side, purl to the yarnover, then p2tog the yarnover with the stitch after gap. Repeat for each yarnover as you work to the end of the row.

*Working in a stitch pattern*
For both right side and wrong side rows, continuing in stitch pattern when possible, work to the point where the short row begins. Turn work.

If the first stitch is a knit stitch, a brk, or a sl 1 or sl1yo that resembles the V of a knit stitch, bring yarn to the front between needles, then work the stitch, forming the yarnover beside it.

If the first stitch is a purl stitch, a brp, or a sl 1 or sl1yo that resembles the ridge of a purl stitch, bring yarn to the back between needles, then work the stitch, forming the yarnover beside it.

After completing your short rows, each yarnover is decreased with the stitch that follows the gap created by the turn. The decrease used to close the gaps will make these short rows invisible on the right side, regardless of whether they are knit stitches or purls.

On the right side, work each yarnover together with the stitch after gap, using k2tog if a knit stitch or p2tog if a purl.

On the wrong side, work each yarnover together with the stitch after gap, using ssk if a knit stitch or ssp if a purl.

# brioche stitches

## Sl1yo before a brk or knit stitch:
Bring the yarn to the front, between the needles, then slip the next stitch purlwise. Bring the yarn over the needle, to the back, ready to knit the next stitch (creates a yarn over traveling over a slipped stitch).

**brk (brioche knit):** Knit the next stitch together with its yarnover.

**brp (brioche purl):** Purl the next st together with its yarnover.

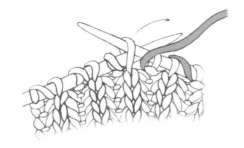

## Sl1yo before a brp or purl stitch:
With the yarn in front, slip the next stitch purlwise. Bring the yarn over the needle, to the back, then between the needles to the front, ready to purl the next stitch (creates a yarn over traveling over a slipped stitch).

# lifted stitch

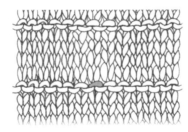

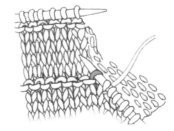

Insert RH needle tip, from the bottom up, into the purl stitch 6 rows below next stitch on needle.

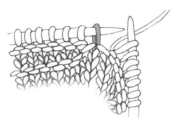

Lift the stitch onto the LH needle.

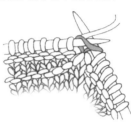

Knit the lifted stitch (see above), knit the next stitch…

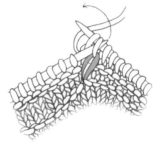

then pass the lifted stitch over it.

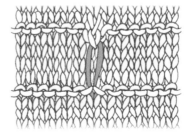

The lifted stitch in pattern.

## beginning a sleeve from a waste yarn cast on

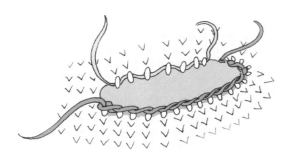

Place your sweater with the sleeve opening laid out flat before you, so that the waste yarn cast on is facing up.

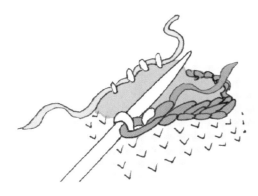

Insert needle tip from front to back into the first stitch (waste yarn is coming from the center of the stitch).

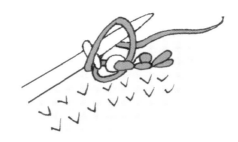

Carefully pick the waste yarn out of the stitch just placed on needle, drawing the tail first back through the stitch to the right,

then down from the center of the next cast on stitch,

and finally through the stitch again, this time to the left, until it is completely removed from the stitch.

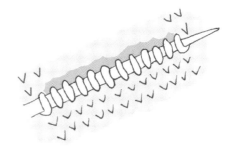

Continue in this manner, one stitch at a time, until all stitches have been placed on needle and waste yarn is removed completely.

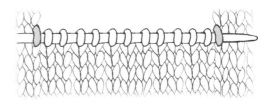

There will be one more stitch on the needle than the number of stitches you cast on. This is because the first and last stitch cast on each "borrow" a leg from a stitch that continued on when working from the body into the yoke on your sweater.

# special abbreviations

**m1 (make 1):** Insert LH needle from front to back under horizontal strand between stitch just worked and next stitch, knit lifted strand through the back loop (1 stitch increased).

**m1-p (make 1 purlwise):** Insert LH needle from front to back under horizontal strand between stitch just worked and next stitch, purl lifted strand through the back loop (1 stitch increased).

**M1R (make 1 right slanting):** Insert LH needle from back to front under horizontal strand between stitch just worked and next stitch, knit lifted strand through the front loop (1 stitch increased).

**M1L (make 1 left slanting):** Insert LH needle from front to back under horizontal strand between stitch just worked and next stitch, knit lifted strand through the back loop (1 stitch increased).

**k1-f/b (knit 1, front and back):** Knit into the front loop, then the back loop of next stitch (1 stitch increased).

**yo (yarn over):** Bring yarn between needles to the front, then over RH needle ready to knit the next stitch (1 stitch increased).

**yo2:** Bring yarn over needle twice. On the next row, work into the first yarn over, dropping the second from the needle (1 stitch increased).

**k2tog:** Knit 2 stitches together (1 stitch decreased, leans to the right).

**ssk (slip, slip, knit):** Slip 2 stitches one at a time knitwise to the RH needle; return stitches to LH needle in turned position and knit them together through the back loops (1 stitch decreased, leans to the left).

**p2tog:** Purl 2 stitches together (1 stitch decreased).

**p2tog-tbl:** Purl 2 stitches together through the back loops (1 stitch decreased).

**ssp (slip, slip, purl):** Slip 2 stitches one at a time knitwise to the RH needle; return stitches to LH needle in turned position and purl them together through the back loops (1 stitch decreased).

**br-ssk (brioche slip, slip, knit):** Slip the next 2 stitches, along with corresponding yarn over, one at a time knitwise to the RH needle; return stitches to LH needle in turned position and knit them together through the back loops (1 stitch decreased, slants to the left).

**br-sssk (brioche slip, slip, slip, knit):** Slip the next 3 stitches, along with corresponding yarn overs, one at a time knitwise to the RH needle; return stitches to LH needle in turned position and knit them together through the back loops (2 stitches decreased, slants to the left).

**br-k3tog (brioche knit three together):** Knit next 3 stitches together, along with corresponding yarn overs (2 stitches decreased, slants to the right).

# standard abbreviations

| | |
|---|---|
| approx | approximately |
| beg | begin(ning); begin; begins |
| BO | bind off |
| BOR | beginning of round |
| CO | cast on |
| CC | contrasting color |
| circ | circular needle |
| cm | centimeter(s) |
| cn | cable needle |
| cont | continue(s); continuing |
| dec('d) | decrease(d) |
| dpn(s) | double-pointed needle(s) |
| est | establish(ed) |
| g | gram(s) |
| inc('d) | increase(d) |
| k | knit |
| LH | left hand |
| MC | main color |
| meas | measures |
| mm | millimeter(s) |
| m | marker(s) |
| p | purl |
| patt(s) | pattern(s) |
| pc(s) | piece(s) |
| pm | place marker |
| rem | remain(ing) |
| rep | repeat; repeating |
| RH | right hand |
| rib | ribbing |
| rnd(s) | round(s) |
| RS | right side |
| sl | slip |
| sl m | slip marker |
| st(s) | stitch(es) |
| tog | together |
| WS | wrong side |
| yd | yard(s) |

# history & bio

Quince & Co is a handknitting yarn and knitwear design company launched in 2010 by Pam Allen in partnership with a historic spinning mill in Maine. Our goal is to work as much as possible with American fibers and mills and, when we can't have a yarn made to our specifications in the US, we look for suppliers overseas who make yarn in as earth- and labor-friendly a way as possible.

Quince began with a core line of five wool yarns—Finch, Chickadee, Lark, Osprey, and Puffin—each with its own personality, each in 37 colors, and all spun in the US from American wool. Today Quince & Co's core line comes in more than 60 colors and we've added Tern, a silk/wool blend, Owl, an alpaca/wool blend, Piper, a super fine mohair/merino blend sourced specifically from Texas, and Willet, a cotton yarn sourced from a Cleaner Cotton™ grower in California. In addition, Quince makes two organic linen yarns, Sparrow and Kestrel, with a mill in Italy. Find out more at www.quinceandco.com.

Pam Allen has worked in the knitting industry for many years as an independent hand-knitwear designer, editor-in-chief of *Interweave Knits* magazine, and creative director at Classic Elite Yarns. She is the author of *Knitting for Dummies* (John Wiley & Sons, 2002), *Scarf Style* (Interweave Press, 2004), and *Home: 18 Knittable Projects to Keep You Comfy* (Quince & Co, 2014).

# acknowledgements

Thanks to:
*Dawn Catanzaro* for managing the tasks, keeping logs, figuring out where to go from wherever we (I) got stuck, for tech editing, knitting, and for invaluable help at the shoot,
*Jerusha Robinson* who never loses her cool, always knows where things are, and who makes the schedule possible,
*Whitney Hayward* for beautiful photography, for making photos of yarn that you can feel with your eyes,
*Leila Raabe* for the lovely technical illustrations,
*Bristol Ivy* for keen-eyed proofreading,
*Kate Novak* of Maggie, Inc for modeling,
*Ryan FitzGerald* for encouraging the book,

and, as always, to the smart, talented, dedicated, and hard-working crew at Quince & Co for making Quince & Co the place that it is.

We're also grateful to Bliss (blissboutiques.com) in Portland, ME, for their generosity in lending us clothes for styling, and to Wolfe Neck Preserve in Freeport, ME for the use of the Mallett Barn.